CLASSIC NATURAL HISTORY PRINTS

MAMMALS

ACKNOWLEDGMENTS

The author and publishers would like to thank the following for their help in the compilation of this book:
The National Museums of Scotland: Andrew Kitchener and David Heppell of the Department of Natural History; the Head of Library, Manjil V. Mathew and his staff. The Natural History Museum, London: the Head of Library Services, Rex Banks and his staff. The Linnean Society of London: the Council and Librarian, Gina Douglas. Ken Smith Photography (Edinburgh). Cavendish House, Carlisle: Una Dance, Robert Dance.

They would also like to thank the following for their kind permission to photograph the original prints in their possession:
The National Museums of Scotland, Edinburgh, for the plates appearing on pages 13, 27, 29, 31, 35, 37, 39, 41, 79, 93, 95, 97, 99, 101, 103, 105, 107, 109, 111, 113, 115, 117, 119, 121, 123, 125, 127. The Natural History Museum, London, for the plates appearing on pages 9, 11, 23, 33, 43, 45, 47, 49, 51, 53, 55, 57, 59, 61, 63, 65, 67, 69, 71, 89 and 91. The Linnean Society of London, for the plates appearing on pages 15, 17, 19, 21, 25, 73, 75, 77, 81 and 83. Una Dance, for the plates appearing on pages 85 and 87.

Classic Natural History Prints, *Mammals*
first published in 1990 by Studio Editions Ltd.
Princess House, 50 Eastcastle Street,
London W1N 7AP, England.

This 1990 edition published by Arch Cape Press,
distributed by Outlet Book Company, Inc.,
a Random House Company,
225 Park Avenue South,
New York, New York 10003.

Printed and bound in Italy

ISBN 0 517 02731 3

h g f e d c b a

CLASSIC NATURAL HISTORY PRINTS

MAMMALS

PHASCOLARCTOS CINEREUS.

S. PETER DANCE

ARCH CAPE PRESS
NEW YORK

INTRODUCTION   5

LIST OF PLATES

European Hedgehog	9	Long-tailed Weasel	69
Moose	11	Northern Flying Squirrel	71
Ring-tailed Lemur	13	Orang Utan	73
Indian Rhinoceros	15	Eland and Guanaco	75
Golden-headed Tamarin	17	Burchell's Zebra	77
Bactarian Camel	19	Gorilla	79
Quagga	21	Maned Wolf	81
Spotted Cuscus	23	Mule Deer	83
Nubian Ibex	25	Pale-throated Sloth	85
Puma	27	Red Howler	87
Capybara	29	Chimpanzee	89
White Whale	31	Hippopotamus	91
Wild Cat	33	Giant Panda	93
Numbat	35	Sumatran Rhinoceros	95
Giraffe	37	Caribbean Manatee	97
Asiatic Elephant	39	Common Dolphin and Bottle-nosed Dolphin	99
Greater Kudu	41	Lion	101
Gemsbok	43	Snow Leopard	103
African Buffalo	45	Clouded Leopard	105
Brown Bear	47	Serval	107
Slender-tailed Cloud Rat	49	Husky Dog	109
Arab Horse	51	Mexican Lap-dog	111
Hereford Cattle	53	Black Wilderbeest and Grant's Gazzelle	113
Lincoln Longwool Sheep	55	European Bison	115
Hog-nosed Skunk	57	Markhor	117
Koala	59	Okapi	119
Thylacine	61	Crested Porcupine	121
Wallaroo	63	Harp Seal	123
Grey-headed Flying Fox	65	Polecat	125
Eastern Chipmunk	67	Blue Whale and Fin Whale	127

INDEX   *128*

INTRODUCTION

One day in September 1940 four lads from the little town of Montignac in south-western France scrambled through a small hole in a wooded plateau and found themselves in an underground cave. Returning the next day with a makeshift light they re-entered the cave and boggled at figures of strange animals, outlined in black and coloured with vivid reds and earthy browns, sprawling across the walls and ceilings. They had stumbled upon the Lascaux cave system and its wonderful series of palaeolithic paintings.

The discovery of this subterranean art gallery showed that, about 25,000 years before the Christian era, some of our ancestors had learnt to make bold, identifiable and life-like portraits of the larger animals sharing their environment. But were they drawn from life? One or two zoologists have argued that most must have been portraits of dead animals; and the way some are shown as though on tip-toe, an attitude they would never have adopted in life, supports that argument. But this does not diminish the stupendous artistic achievement of the troglodytes. The beasts portrayed so unforgettably in their gloomy cave must have meant a great deal to the ancient image makers of Lascaux.

Early civilisations in both East and West have left evidence of a widespread enthusiasm for animal art in one form or another. From Mesopotamia we have cylinder seals carved with lions and other animals dating from about 2000 BC. From China we have representations of a variety of animals carved into objects made from jade, marble, pottery and bronze dating from the same period. About 1500 BC paintings of domestic animals became a common feature of the civilisation of the New Kingdom in Egypt; and colossal stone lions and human-headed bulls characterised the might of the Assyrian empire. By then dolphins and other marine creatures were familiar motifs on pottery and on palace walls at Knossos in Crete when the Minoan culture was at its zenith. Austere but well-proportioned horses from the Parthenon typify Greek art of the millenium before the birth of Christ; and the sprightly animal portraits seen on wall paintings and mosaics unearthed from the ashes which buried Pompeii epitomise the very different, life-enhancing attitude to animals adopted later by the Romans.

So, thousands of years before the prints reproduced in this book appeared, the urge to make images of horses, lions, dolphins, bulls and other large mammals had been expressed in various and often wonderful ways. Further expressions of that urge may be seen in sculptures, carvings, hanging scrolls and illuminated manuscripts fashioned by artists of various cultures up to the time of the Renaissance. In Europe the first prints to portray animals were products of that time.

Some of the finest of the earliest prints of mammals produced in Europe were the work of the outstanding Renaissance artist Albrecht Dürer. His scientific approach to graphic art ensured that a drawing of a hare or a horse was minutely correct – although he was guilty of superimposing a tiny unicorn's horn on the back of a now famous study of an Indian rhinoceros. The woodcuts in Conrad Gessner's mid-sixteenth-century publication *Historia Animalium* were less scrupulously exact (many of them represented exotic creatures known only from their dead remains, from inadequate sketches or from hearsay) but became very popular and were still being reproduced in books two centuries later. During the seventeenth century many more woodcuts of animals appeared in books devoted to aspects of natural history but, with few exceptions, they were no more accurate and often aesthetically less pleasing than Gessner's. Unless specially commissioned, none of these publications was issued with the woodcuts coloured by hand; that was an eighteenth-century development.

Dürer had shown that the most accurate and most satisfying pictures of animals were those based on a close scrutiny of the animals themselves: so for a long time the best animal pictures were those of domestic subjects. Pictures of exotic animals were likely to be unsatisfactory by comparison because the subjects were scarce or in poor condition; and sometimes the artist had only inferior sketches, inadequate notes or oral descriptions to work from. In a European context, therefore, an artist could not produce a satisfactory portrait of, say, a lion, an elephant or a monkey unless he had access to a menagerie. Alternatively, it was sometimes possible to gain access to preserved skins or mounted specimens in private collections of natural curiosities (there were no public ones before the middle of the eighteenth century), such as those amassed by the Englishman Hans Sloane and the Dutchman Albert Seba.

Sloane's collection eventually formed the nucleus of that in the British Museum; Seba sold his first collection to Peter the Great of Russia and his second was dispersed, but not before it had been described and illustrated in a massive four-volume book, now known as Seba's *Thesaurus*. The first plate in our own book comes from the copy of the *Thesaurus* owned formerly by Sloane, a copy specially hand coloured for him, and shows various hedgehogs from Seba's extensive collection. While artists worked from this kind of material their portraits of mammals and other animals were certain to be lifeless; and for most of the eighteenth century lifeless they were.

The *Histoire Naturelle des Mammifères* by E. Geoffroy Saint-Hilaire and G. F. Cuvier, published early in the nineteenth century, was the first large-scale illustrated treatise on mammals. Its hand coloured engravings were reproductions of drawings by highly accomplished artists employed to help professional naturalists working at the Jardin des Plantes in Paris. The engravings, three of which are reproduced here, were sensitively drawn and well coloured, but they showed mammals as though they were precious works of art displayed in an art gallery rather than animals made of flesh and blood shown against natural backgrounds. C. G. Ehrenberg's sensitive illustration of several Nubian ibex in their rocky stronghold, published in 1828, contrasts strikingly with the polished but static French illustrations of mammals published at about the same time. The engravings in James Wilson's *Illustrations of Zoology*, most of them by William Home Lizars (who engraved the first few plates of John James Audubon's *The Birds of America*), were also more lively, if occasionally less original than their French counterparts.

The invention of lithography, a process allowing prints to be taken from a design drawn directly onto a smooth stone surface and inked, came into commercial use in the 1820s. Our picture of the Bactrian camel, from the *Histoire Naturelle des Mammifères*, is an early example of its application to natural history illustration. By the late 1830s lithography had become the principal method used to illustrate the larger animals, the soft lines and subtle shadings of the process helping the artist to capture the essence of fur and feathers. The resulting prints had to be coloured by hand, in the same way as steel engravings, and even when colouring by the automatic process known as chromo-lithography came into general use in the second half of the century, hand coloured lithographs still illustrated the more expensive natural history books.

Lithography was not only speedier than other processes such as engraving on steel or wood, it was cheaper and easier to master. Soon it became the preferred method of illustrating the larger animals (it was less suitable when applied to smaller creatures such as insects, the lines being too coarse to define their more delicate structures). Here was a graphic reproduction process which could be used to illustrate some of the new and unusual creatures which travellers and explorers were bringing to Europe in large numbers from Africa, South America, India, Indonesia and other places rich in wildlife. As well as institutions such as the Jardin des Plantes in Paris and the Gardens of the Zoological Society in London, the private residences of wealthy men, such as the Earl of Derby's seat at Knowsley Hall near Liverpool, now often included menageries and aviaries crowded with exotic creatures. Animal artists could visit these establishments and make sketches of their living inhabitants and, soon afterwards perhaps, lithographs of their finished pictures could be in the hands of the colourists. It was not usually as simple as this, of course; to turn out a series of hand coloured lithographs of high quality required great skill and patience.

Lithography caught on quickly in the United States and, in Europe, only the French seemed slow to adopt it. While steel engravings illustrated the scientific reports of the French research vessels *Venus* and *Bonite* in the 1840s, the British in particular were busy publishing natural history works, some of them substantial, illustrated by lithography. David Low used the process with telling effect to illustrate his folio book *The Breeds of the Domestic Animals of the British Islands*. John Gould, well known for his series of magnificently illustrated bird books, all illustrated with lithographs, found time to bring out an equally impressive work, *The Mammals of Australia*. In the United States John James Audubon and the Revd John Bachman emulated Gould by describing and illustrating the entire mammal fauna of North America in their monumental publication *The Viviparous Quadrupeds of North America*. (Curiously, the scientific reports of the United States Exploring Expedition, including the *Mammalogy and Ornithology* report published in 1858, were illustrated with steel engravings, but these had probably been prepared long before publication.)

A series of folio-sized lithographs, from original drawings by Benjamin Waterhouse Hawkins, illustrating mammals then on display in the Earl of Derby's menagerie, were published in 1850. The three lithographs from the series reproduced here show that Hawkins had an excellent understanding of mammalian anatomy and pictorial composition. Other lithographs from the series, however, portray mammals with large, liquid eyes reminiscent of those we associate with heroines of Victorian melodramas. No one could say this about the mammal portraits executed by Joseph Wolf, one of the most outstanding of all wildlife artists, whose original drawings were ideal for reproduction by lithography.

Wolf produced the original watercolour drawings for many lithographs of mammals, perhaps the finest of them being those reproduced in Daniel Giraud Elliot's book, *A Monograph of the Felidae, or Family of the Cats*, published in 1883. Wolf's career as a wildlife artist, however, had begun many years before in his native Germany and he had been commissioned to produce illustrations for books, especially bird books, as early as 1830.

His subjects, whatever their place of origin, are always well observed and usually shown in naturalistic settings. It is difficult to believe that Wolf had never seen most of the exotic creatures he drew so skilfully in their native haunts: but the London Zoo provided him with endless opportunities to examine and sketch creatures from parts of the world inaccessible to him; and he used his fertile but disciplined imagination to place them in their own wild environment. Often he had only a single beast as his model but he could multiply it wonderfully to create a family group or a herd. As our picture of a Sumatran rhinoceros shows, he could bring together in the same picture two animals which had never met; even trick photography could not produce a more satisfactory illusion of togetherness. In the nineteenth century Joseph Wolf had no peer; and although the twentieth has produced wildlife artists who display a wonderful ability to present wild animals in all their moods and in every conceivable setting, they all owe something to him, for he showed them the way.

Most of the prints reproduced in this book have been chosen because they are aesthetically pleasing; a few have been included because of some oddity or special charm. Inevitably, most of the mammals portrayed are large and attractive, whereas most mammal species are small and inconspicuous: so it is important to be able to see the selected subjects in relation to the rest of the mammalian world. A few statistics will help to put things into perspective.

About 4231 mammal species are now living or have recently become extinct. Carnivores, which provide us with the subjects of some of our most compelling illustrations, such as bears, big cats, dogs and seals, account for about 266 of them. What are known as the even-toed ungulates, comprising such well known animals as deer, cattle, antelopes, camels, pigs, giraffes and hippopotamus, account for about 192 species. The primates, including lemurs, baboons, monkeys, great apes and ourselves, comprise at most a further 181 species. These groups, well represented in our 60 illustrative plates, make up roughly a seventh of the world total. Most of the remainder are small and inconspicuous animals.

The rodents, for example, number about 1738 species. Of these about 1120 comprise the *Muridae*, the family containing mice, rats, voles and their allies; this book includes only one member of this family, a rat, but it may claim to be the world's largest rat. When hunting for pictures suitable for inclusion in this book it seemed that those of squirrels (which are rodents) and their allies outnumbered all others. As there are about 255 different kinds on several continents, many of them widespread and abundant, it is not surprising that there should have been so many illustrations of them in the earlier natural history books. Because they are monotonously similar and often drab they do not figure largely in our selection. Unexpectedly, perhaps, there are almost a thousand species of bats in the world. Bats, too, all look much the same as each other and only one, an Australian flying fox, finds a place here. Mice and rats, squirrels and bats, all have their place in nature, but in this book they have had to make way for those mammals which are large, impressive, historically interesting or simply odd.

Sometimes the oddness is less evident in the mammals themselves than in the artists' portraits of them. John James Audubon often dramatised his pictures of birds and mammals to emphasise the harsh realities of nature, red in tooth and claw, but his illustration of the eastern chipmunk shows a little fellow with its mouth full of nuts looking as though it has escaped from an animated cartoon.

Oddest of all in our selection are the two colour printed engravings taken from *The Instructive Picture Book* by an unknown author, dating from 1860. One is meant to show figures of pale-throated sloths, while the other supposedly shows us figures of the red howler monkey. But the sloths have the

INTRODUCTION

beguiling faces of displaced nuns and the monkeys are acting the parts of Adam and Eve! Such pictorial curiosities, whatever hidden meanings may lurk behind them, deserve to be rescued from oblivion if only to show us how an unknown artist's vision differed from ours.

Among the more memorable images in this small gallery of mammal pictures is the first credible group portrait of the lowland gorilla, one of Wolf's most sensitive studies. Here, too, is the first published illustration of the giant panda, a remarkable achievement as it was almost certainly based upon a preserved skin of a specimen taken to Paris shortly after its discovery in central China by the missionary Père David. Even more remarkable is P. J. Smit's fine 1902 lithograph of the okapi, the first published figure of a creature which was then a new and exciting discovery. Although it gives the impression of being a portrait of the living animal it was actually a reconstruction based on a skin and some other fragmentary remains which had been brought to London from the Congo. Of importance in a different context are the three lithographs taken from David Low's authoritative book, *The Breeds of the Domestic Animals of the British Islands*. Had Low not taken the trouble to publish such pictures in 1842 it would now be difficult or impossible to reconstruct the appearance of some of these breeds.

The pictures reproduced here and many others like them provide invaluable evidence of the appearance of mammals as they were (or were supposed to be) many years ago: but they are more than factual records. They allow us to view a vanished part of the natural world as if through the eyes of the artists who made the pictures, although this may require some effort on our part. We should realise, for instance, that artists did not always see mammals and other animals as we do now. Seldom, for instance, did they represent their subjects other than broadside on, James Wilson's capybara stands out as a rare exception. For many years, too, they often failed to inject life into their subjects. The studies published by Audubon and Bachman, however, occasionally inject too much of it.

Most artists must have some kind of training if they are to succeed as artists. Those who executed the pictures reproduced here received a very different training to that given to artists now. Their models were usually static and they were seldom encouraged to express their own individualism. As often as not the animals they drew or painted were dead; sometimes they were literally no more than skin and bones.

Today's wildlife artists would not accept such constraints. The material and educational advantages such artists now enjoy should not be taken for granted; they are better equipped than their predecessors in almost every way. In one respect, however, they are at a distinct disadvantage. Some of the animals they would like to have seen in the wild or even in captivity, such as one or two of those portrayed in our selection, are now no more. We should be grateful for the pictorial legacy bequeathed to us by yesterday's wildlife artists. Some of their work, by any standard, was excellent, some of it pedestrian: but it was all worthwhile.

Knowing that some of the animals portrayed by these artists will never be seen alive again has helped us to understand that the animals which remain mean a great deal to us. We may not realise it, but we are close in spirit to the image-makers of Lascaux.

[7]

European Hedgehog

PETIT HERISSON (now European Hedgehog, *Erinaceus europaeus*) and other Hedgehogs. Hand coloured engraving by P. Tanjé, pl. 49 from Vol. 1 of A. Seba's *Locupletissimi Rerum Naturalium Thesauri Accurata Descriptio &c*, 1734–65. Size of plate 17¼″ × 11″.

At the beginning of the eighteenth century the Amsterdam apothecary, Albert Seba, assembled a large collection of dried plants, stuffed animals, shells, insects and other natural curiosities. He sold it to Peter the Great of Russia in 1717 and then assembled another, even larger collection which he kept. Seba often acquired exotic specimens from seamen newly arrived from distant lands as payment for his professional services, but he did not disdain to add to his stores specimens of the commoner animals of Europe, such as the European hedgehog (illustrated by the two figures at the top of this plate). The white hedgehog in the centre of the plate was said to have been sent to Seba from Surinam in South America and to have been regarded by the 'Indians' there as 'delicious to eat'. As hedgehogs are not native to South America this white hedgehog must have originated elsewhere.

Although the European hedgehog is host to many different kinds of parasite, such as fleas and ticks, it was formerly esteemed a delicacy among country folk. In a fourteenth-century German treatise about natural history, Konrad von Megengerg wrote, 'the flesh of the hedgehog is wholesome for the stomach and strengthens the same. Likewise it hath a power of drying and relieving the stomach. It deals with the water of dropsy and is of great help to such as are inclined to the sickness called elephantiasis'. Its own sense of taste is well developed: given a choice, it prefers food with a characteristic flavour. An ancient fable would have us believe that it will roll on to windfall apples, impale them on its spines and carry them off to its nest. Although this extraordinary notion still receives an occasional airing it is not supported by any well attested proof.

TAB. XLIX.

Fig. 1.

Fig. 2.

Fig. 3.

Fig. 4.

Fig. 5.

Moose

ELK, *Cervus alces* (now Moose, *Alces alces*). Hand coloured engraving by J. F. Miller, pl. 10 from his *Icones Animalium* (or *Various Subjects of Natural History*, 1776–85. Size of plate 17½″ × 11½″.

This engraving is from one of the rarest of eighteenth-century natural history books. Most of the few surviving copies of John Frederick Miller's *Icones Animalium* are incomplete and all are inaccessible to the general public; even now bibliographers disagree about the book's contents and publication dates. Fortunately the engravings included in it were re-issued in 1796, together with an explanatory text, under the title *Cimelia Physica*. Miller, who worked for Sir Joseph Banks, was more at home with plants than animals, so there is a naive quality about this representation of the largest living deer.

The scientific (genus) name of this bulky animal, *Alces*, is from the Greek word for elk, the name by which the moose is known in Europe. Widespread in northern North America, the moose varies considerably in size, the Alaskan form standing over six feet at the shoulder, weighing up to 1200 pounds or more and sporting enormous, spoon-shaped antlers. By comparison, the antlers of the European forms are much smaller and more flattened. The moose is usually a solitary animal and in summer feeds in low-lying swampy districts and at lakesides. In winter it moves into wooded areas and feeds on leaves, shoots and tender branches. The long, coarse hair provides a coat which helps to insulate the moose against the bitterly cold temperatures of the northern winters. Its great size makes it an easy target for hunters, but it has managed to survive over a considerable part of the northern hemisphere.

TAB. X.

Printed Engrav'd and Publish'd according to the Act by I.F. Miller 1796.

Ring-tailed Lemur

Le Mococo, *Lemur catta* (now Ring-tailed Lemur, *Lemur catta*). Colour printed engraving by J. B. Audebert, pl. 4 (of *Makis*) from his *Histoire Naturelle des Singes et des Makis*, 1799–1800. Size of plate 20″ × 13″.

Jean Baptiste Audebert was one of several outstanding French artists whose illustrations signalled a new and splendid epoch in the history of animal portraiture at the beginning of the nineteenth century. The attitude of the tail in this study of a ring-tailed lemur is so characteristic of the animal that Audebert probably drew from a captive specimen, not from a preserved skin.

Madagascar is the natural home of nearly all the lemurs, most of which live in trees. Audebert correctly shows his ring-tailed lemur on the ground where it lives amongst rocks in the southern part of the island, the black and white rings on its tail distinguishing it from all other lemurs. When not looking for its food, which consists of various kinds of fruit, birds' eggs and insects, it spends most of its time cleaning and licking the fur of other members of its own species. It is usual for the young to cling tightly to the underside of their mother for the first three weeks; afterwards they ride about on her back. When disturbed or worried it will adopt a crouching posture with its tail covering its breast and in this position will run its tail repeatedly through its arms. At the same time it spreads onto its tail secretions from scent glands on its wrists and shoulder region. It is still common in the wild and is the most familiar species of its family in captivity.

Pl. 4

Le Mococo. Buff.

Audebert pinx. et sculp.   Lemur Catta. Linn.   Finot Imp.

Indian Rhinoceros

RHINOCEROS UNICORN (now Indian Rhinoceros, *Rhinoceros unicornis*). Hand coloured engraving, unnumbered plate from Vol. 1 of E.G. Saint-Hilaire and G. F. Cuvier's *Histoire Naturelle des Mammifères*, 1819. Size of plate 20″ × 13″.

There are five different species of rhinoceros living today. The largest of the three Asiatic species, and the best known, is the Indian rhinoceros, which is now restricted to grassy areas and jungles in Bengal, Assam, and Nepal. Weighing in at more than two tons, standing six feet at the shoulder and fourteen feet long, the male Indian rhinoceros is not to be trifled with (although its vital statistics are exceeded by those of the white rhinoceros of Africa which is normally larger and has tipped the scales at five tons).

Unlike the African rhinos it has only one horn, present in both sexes and rather short and blunt. Compensating for the inadequacy of its horn as a weapon there is a pair of sharp-edged incisor tusks in the lower jaw, with which it slashes at a potential enemy. It is peace-loving, retiring and solitary by nature and so is unlikely to attack unless provoked.

This view of the Indian rhinoceros displays its characteristically folded and knobbly hide. These features are emphasised in the earliest published illustration of the animal by a western artist, Albert Dürer, which was based on a sketch of a living animal seen and sketched at Lisbon in 1515. Not only did he represent the hide as though it were armour plating, he also gave the Lisbon beast a tiny extra horn on its back behind the head, an embellishment usually reserved for representations of the fabulous unicorn. Nevertheless, Dürer's fanciful picture has been reproduced countless times since his day and is still a popular image of the Indian rhinoceros; such is the power of a great artist.

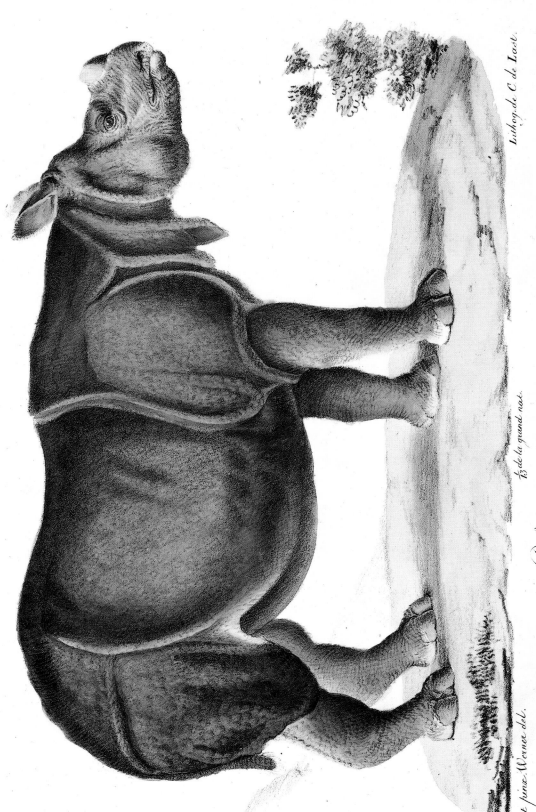

Huet pinx. Werner del.

Lithog. de C. de Last.

⅓ de la grand. nat.

Rhinocéros unicorne.

Golden-headed Tamarin

LE SAHUI NOIR, *Hapale chrysomelas* (now Golden-headed Tamarin, *Leonto-pithecus chrysomelas*). Hand coloured engraving, pl. 9 from Part 2 of Prince Maximilian Alexander Philipp of Wied-Neuwied's *Recueil de Planches Col-oriées d'Animaux du Brésil*, 1822–31. Size of plate 10½″ × 9″.

This engraving contrasts strangely with modern illustrations of the golden-headed tamarin, a small South American primate. The tamarins are noted for the mane of long, silky fur around their shoulders but it does not stand up so dramatically as this picture suggests. As this was one of the first, if not the first, published illustration of it and was probably an artist's reconstruction based on a preserved skin we should not be too critical. A small animal, it travels in small groups and leaps from branch to branch with great agility. It shelters in hollow trees and crevices and feeds upon fruit, insects, lizards and probably birds' eggs.

Prince Maximilian led an expedition into the interior of Brazil in the early nineteenth century and said in his published report that this creature often provided him and his colleagues with a meal. He also said that if it could survive the rigours of a voyage to Europe it would 'truly be an ornament in our rooms'; in other words it would make an amusing pet for those in fashionable society. It is not likely to make a pet in our own day because, like the other two golden tamarins of eastern Brazil, it is in danger of being exterminated. In 1981 the total population was estimated at less than 200 specimens. As the destruction of its habitat continues and collectors hunt it to stock zoos there is little likelihood of it surviving for very long in the wild.

Hapale chrysomelas.

9

Bactrian Camel

LE CHAMEAU DE LA BACTRIANE, *Camelus bactrianus* (now Bactrian Camel, *Camelus bactrianus*). Hand coloured lithograph by C. de Last from an original drawing by Werner, unnumbered plate in Part 29, Vol. 2 of E. G. Saint-Hilaire and G.F. Cuvier's *Histoire Naturelle des Mammifères*, 1824. Size of plate 20″ × 13″.

In the early nineteenth century the Bactrian camel may have been less familiar to Europeans than the Arabian camel, *Camelus dromedarius*. This picture of it is probably better than any published earlier, although it tends to idealise the appearance of a creature which loses its thick, brown winter coat in patches. The twin humps, which immediately distinguish it from the single-humped Arabian camel, have no supporting bony structure and are fat storage organs enabling it to survive when food is scarce. The Bactrian camel is the slower of the two and is used primarily as a beast of burden, often travelling in great caravans across the inhospitable, stony deserts and snow-bound wastes of central Asia.

Its popular name is derived from Bactria, the name of an ancient kingdom of eastern Persia which covered an area corresponding roughly to the modern province of Balkh in Afghanistan. The reliefs decorating the walls of Xerxes' palace at Persepolis show tribute bearers leading Bactrian camels, proof enough that these hardy animals have been domesticated for a very long time. Very few truly wild Bactrian camels are alive today.

Werner del.

Lithog. de C. de Lasteyrie

de la grand nat.

Chameau de la Bactriane.

Quagga

LE COUAGGA, *Equus quagga* (now Quagga, *Equus quagga*). Hand coloured lithograph by C. de Last from an original drawing by Werner (an error for Maréchal?), unnumbered plate in Part 30, Vol. 2 of E. G. Saint-Hilaire and G.F. Cuvier's *Histoire Naturelle des Mammifères*, 1824. Size of plate 20″ × 13″.

The quagga has been extinct since 1883 when the last one, an old mare, died at the Amsterdam Zoo. Measuring about four and a half feet high at the shoulder it was one of the smallest of the zebras and resembled a horse more closely than did the others because its stripes did not extend much farther back than the base of its mane. It is sometimes aptly described as having had the rear end of a horse and the front end of a zebra. It did not neigh like a horse, however, the name quagga being derived from its barking noise.

Formerly plentiful on the plains of the southern parts of South Africa, its fate was sealed when the Boers began slaughtering it for its meat and hide. The individual illustrated here lived in the Jardin des Plantes at Paris and died there in 1793. In that year Nicolas Maréchal, an artist who specialised in portrayals of natural history subjects, made a brilliant painting of it on parchment. His painting, now preserved in the National Museum of Natural History in Paris, is evidently the original of this lithograph. At the foot of the lithograph the original painting is attributed to Werner. As Jean Charles Werner was not born until long after the animal depicted had died this attribution must be erroneous.

Maréchal pinx Werner del.

Lith. de C de Last.

♂ de la grand. nat

Couagga.

Spotted Cuscus

PHALANGER TACHETÉ, *Phalangista maculata* (now Spotted Cuscus, *Phalanger maculatus*). Hand coloured engraving by Coutant from an original drawing by Prévost, pl. 7 from the *Atlas* to J. R. C. Quoy and J. P. Gaimard's *Zoologie* (in M. L. de Freycinet's *Voyage autour du Monde . . . sur . . . l'Uranie et la Physicienne*), 1824–26. Size of plate 12½″ × 9½″.

From 1817 to 1820 the French exploring vessels *Uranie* and *Physicienne* went around the world and visited several islands in the Pacific, including Waigeou off the north-western tip of New Guinea. Among the many unusual creatures observed on this tropical island was the spotted cuscus, a tree-living marsupial the size of a domestic cat. At least one example was brought back to Paris to be studied and, eventually, to be immortalised in this rather formal portrait published in the scientific report of the expedition. It is most unlikely that any living examples were taken back to France because the stress involved in capturing and transporting these animals ensures that few survive a long voyage or captivity.

Early travellers would sometimes mistake it for a monkey, partly because it is mainly nocturnal and partly because of their ignorance of marsupials. With its thick, curly coat, furry, prehensile tail and roundish head with large, red-rimmed eyes it would have presented an unusual sight to a traveller seeing it for the first time as it stared out through the thick greenery of its humid forest. It moves about lazily at night, feeding upon leaves and fruit, birds and their eggs or fledglings. During the day it mostly sleeps in the hollows of trees or merely clutches boughs. Of the several colour variants the spotted one seen here is the commonest. Abundant in New Guinea the spotted cuscus is one of the rarer Australian marsupials, being found only in the forests of Cape York Peninsula at the north-eastern extremity of the continent.

3/5 de grandeur.

A. Prévost pinx.^t   Contant sculp.^t

PHALANGER TACHETÉ: *(PHALANGISTA MACULATA. Geoff.)*

Nubian Ibex

Capra sinaitica (now Nubian Ibex, *Capra nubiana*). Hand coloured engraving, pl. 18 from Christian Gottfried Ehrenberg's *Symbolae Physicae. Pars Zoologica, Mammalia*, 1828. Size of plate 19″ × 13″.

This sensitive study captures the noble character of the Nubian ibex and shows that it is a creature of mountainous districts. Virtually a mountain-dwelling wild goat, it displays incredible agility and grace as it bounds from crag to crag, leaps over chasms, and ascends the apparently smooth sides of precipitous slopes. It lives at altitudes of between 600 and 6000 feet above sea level, and is at home in arid, desert country where bare mountains alternate with steep-sided valleys and where rocky outcrops abound; country such as that found in Israel, the Sudan, Sinai, Upper Egypt and Arabia, its collective area of distribution. Apparently impervious to the harshest weather conditions, it never leaves the mountains, finding enough sustenance in the grasses and bushes which constitute the impoverished flora of such an environment.

Although blessed with sharp eyesight and a highly developed sense of smell the Nubian ibex, like the walia ibex, has suffered greatly from the depredations of man, perhaps its only effective enemy. Already of economic importance to the native peoples living in its range (they have always valued it for its flesh, hide, woolly underfur and coarse hair) it has been hunted almost to extinction in recent years. Only a rigorous protection policy will give it a chance to survive. Its fine horns provide hunters with an irresistible incentive to kill it. The horns are not massive but they are longer than those of the walia ibex, measuring more than 40 inches, and are bevelled on the outer front edge, resulting in a narrow front surface. Unfortunately, these majestic ornaments help to make it a conspicuous target.

CAPRA *finaitica.*
Capra nubica F. Cuvier.
in Nubia nunquam visa
ex Aegypto superiore et e montibus
finaiticis.

Mas. adultus, femina adulta et femina juvenis.

F. Bürde fecit.

Puma

PUMA OR AMERICAN LION, *Felis concolor*. Hand coloured engraving by W. H. Lizars, pl. 1 from J. Wilson's *Illustrations of Zoology*, 1831. Size of plate 16″ × 12″.

In October 1826 a frigate from Brazil arrived at Portsmouth, England. On board was a young puma, intended for Robert Jameson's Natural History Museum in the University of Edinburgh. It escaped during a stopover in London but a night watchman recaptured it and it returned to its quarters peaceably. On 8 January 1827 it reached Edinburgh where, after taking a little time to adjust to the climate, it settled down and began to enjoy its new surroundings – a lumber room under the Library of Edinburgh University! Here it became a great attraction for several months, especially to James Wilson who observed it closely.

'It rejoices greatly in the society of those to whose company it is accustomed', he writes, in the text to this plate, 'lies down upon its back between their feet, and plays with the skirts of their garments, entirely after the manner of a kitten. When let loose, it exhibits the most extraordinary feats of activity, springing about in a large lumber room, and assuming an infinite variety of elegant and picturesque positions. It shows a great predilection for water, and frequently jumps into and out of a large tub, rolling itself about, and seeming greatly pleased with the refreshment.' Wilson points out that 'the only animals which have fallen victims to its rapacity, were a mallard drake and a cock pheasant, both of which inadvertently approached within the circle of its spring, and were each killed by a blow of its forepaw' – which at least sounds more like the normal behaviour of a puma.

Traces of the blackish-brown spots which characterise young individuals of this species may still be seen in this portrait, which was obviously done from life. The curious convolutions of the tail were especially noted by Wilson and have been observed in other captive pumas. It seems that this playful animal did not become a stuffed exhibit in Professor Jameson's Museum but may have ended its days quietly in a menagerie elsewhere in Edinburgh, a fitting conclusion to a curiously unconventional life.

PLATE I.

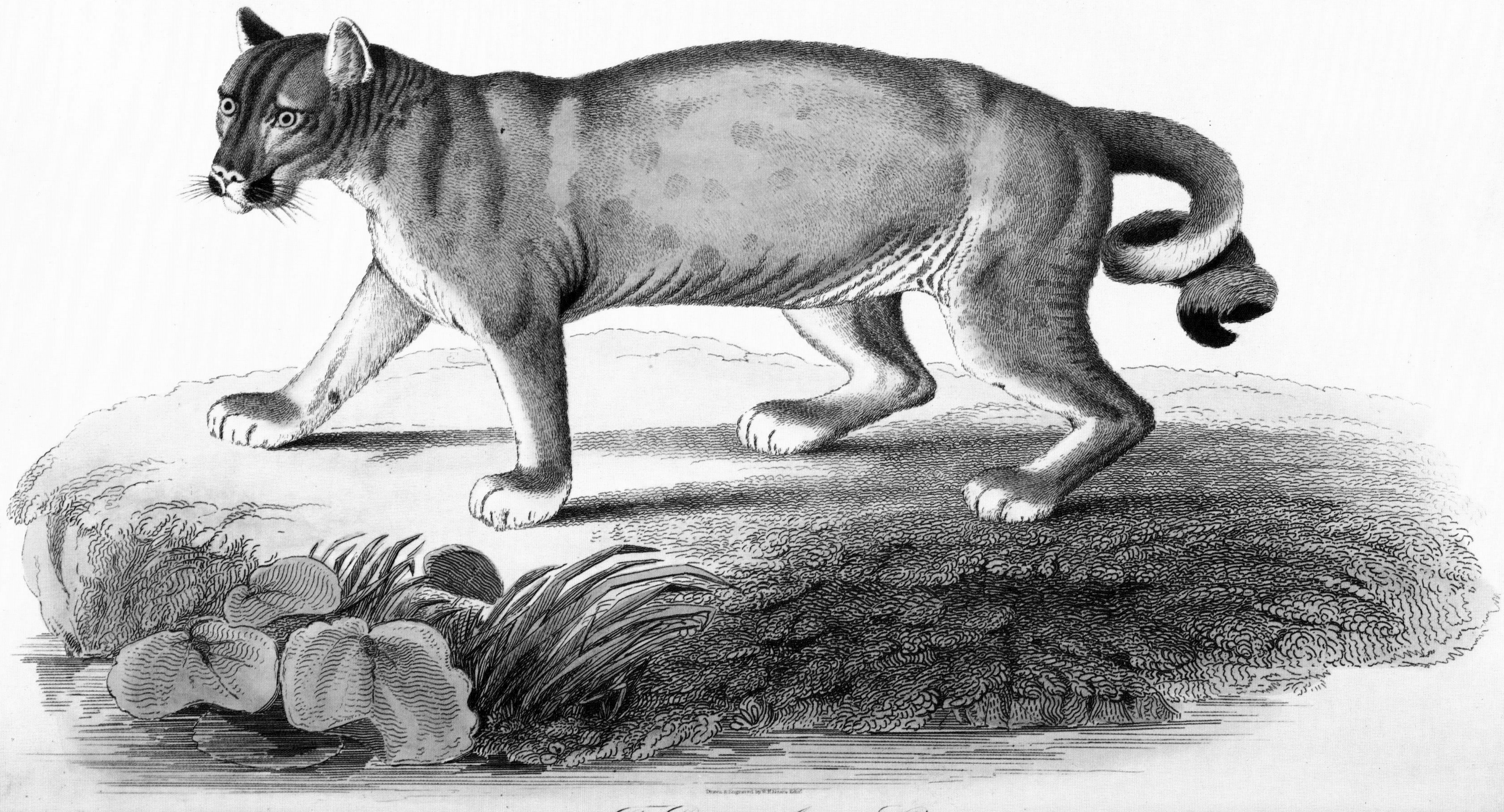

Drawn & Engraved by W. H. Lizars Edin.

The Puma, or American Lion.

Capybara

CAPYBARA OR WATER-HOG, *Hydrochaerus capybara* (now Capybara, *Hydrochoerus hydrochaeris*). Hand coloured engraving by W. H. Lizars from an original drawing by A. Mosses, pl. 13 from J. Wilson's *Illustrations of Zoology*, 1831. Size of plate 16″ × 12″.

The adult capybara, largest of living rodents, is about four feet long, stands about 21 inches tall at the shoulder and may weigh more than 100 pounds. At home in the river networks of South America it grazes on river-bank vegetation and aquatic plants. Although attached to water it may come on to dry land in fine weather to rest and to enjoy the sunshine. It adapts readily to life in captivity and may become very friendly with its captors.

James Wilson, commenting on the figures of the capybara reproduced here, said that they 'were drawn by Mr Mosses of Liverpool, from a full grown female capybara which lived for some months in that town'. He added some curious information about its habits in captivity. 'Its voice was plaintive', he said, 'not unlike that of a newly dropped lamb, and seemed very feeble for so large an animal. It loved human society, and frequently hopped up stairs, and entered the bed-rooms in search of the children of the family, whom it readily followed. The length of its hind legs rendered hopping its easiest motion, and it was capable of considerable bounds. It had the power of erecting all its hair after the manner of the hedge-hog, and its black, scaly skin then became distinctly visible through the thinly set fur. It ate grass, and all sorts of vegetable matters, but seemed to prefer wheaten bread to other diet. When taken to the water, it swam and dived admirably, remained a long time beneath the surface, and quitted its favourite element with reluctance.'

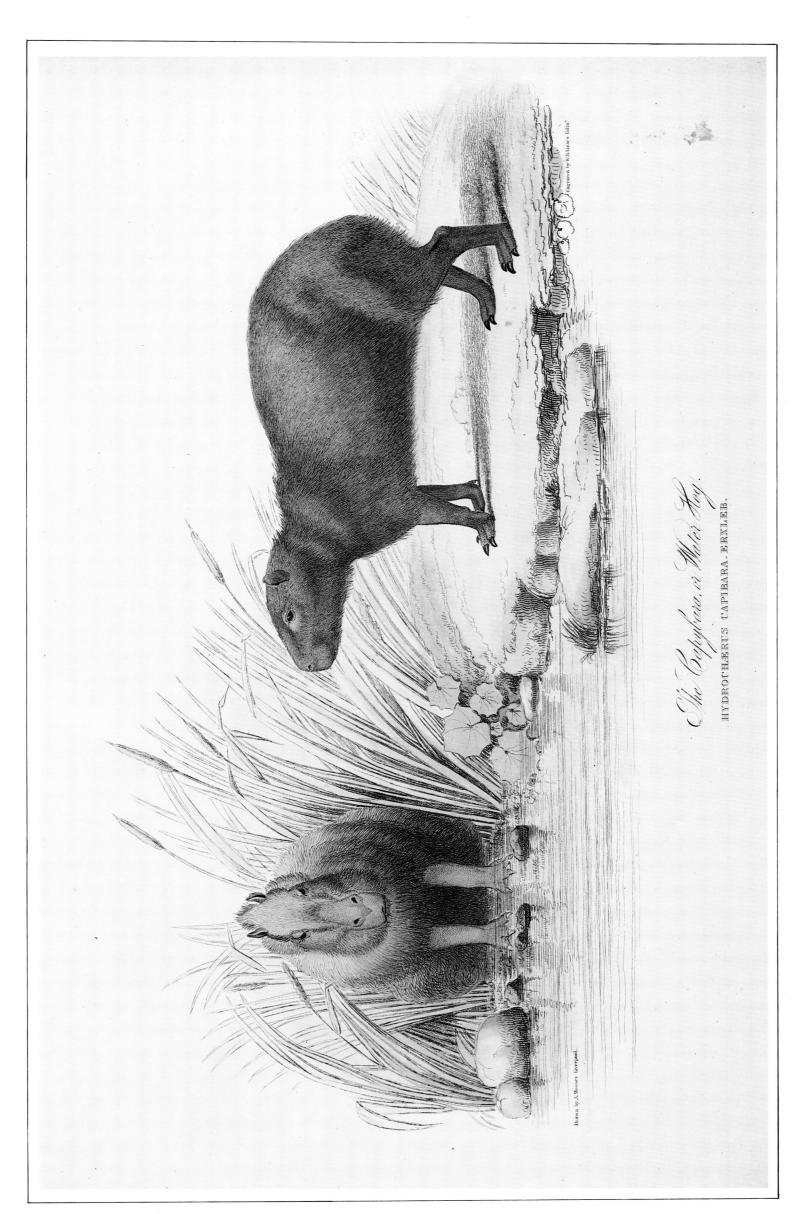

The Capybara, or Water Hog.

HYDROCHÆRUS CAPIBARA. ERXLEB.

Drawn by A. Moses, Liverpool.

Engraved by W.H. Lizars Edin.

White Whale

BELUGA OR GREAT WHITE DOLPHIN, *Delphinapterus beluga* (now White Whale, *Delphinapterus leucas*). Hand coloured engraving by W. H. Lizars from an original drawing by Patrick Syme, pl. 16 from J. Wilson's *Illustrations of Zoology*, 1831. Size of plate 16″ × 12″.

The reason this strange looking creature found its way into James Wilson's *Illustrations of Zoology* is probably because, for about three months in the spring of 1815, it became a talking point among the intelligentsia of Edinburgh, where Wilson worked. Wilson tells us that it 'was observed to inhabit the Firth of Forth, passing upwards almost every day with the tide, and returning again with the ebbing of the waters. It excited great attention by the purity of its colour, and frequent attempts were made to slay or secure it, but without effect, till the 7th of June, when it was killed in the river near Stirling, by means of spears and fire arms. It was purchased by Mr Robert Bald of Alloa, and kindly transmitted by him to Professor Jameson, and on examination was found to be the Beluga of naturalists.' It measured 14 feet 4 inches from the tip of the jaw to the end of the tail, so it was a youngster; this pure white, gentle creature may grow to almost twice this length.

Normally white whales frequent coasts bordering the Arctic Ocean where their white bodies are not easily seen against the ice and snow. Occasionally, however, young examples will swim far up rivers and have even been reported 700 miles up the River Yukon. This gives fishermen a chance to trap and kill them and explains the presence of one in a river near Stirling in Scotland. But how can the presence of an iceberg in the background of Wilson's picture be explained, bearing in mind the geographical position of Stirling? The answer is simple. In 1820, eleven years before Wilson's book was published, William Scoresby had published at Edinburgh *An Account of the Arctic Regions, with a History and Description of the Northern Whale-Fishery*; it includes an engraving of the white whale, complete with iceberg, almost identical with Wilson's. The one Wilson wrote about was not the same as the one he illustrated, but that may have seemed unimportant in 1831.

PLATE XVI.

The Belouga or Great White Dolphin.

DELPHINAPTERUS BELUGA, LACEPEDE.

Drawn by Patrick Syme.

Engd by W.H. Lizars.

Wild Cat

CHAT SAUVAGE, *Felis catus* (now Wild Cat, *Felis silvestris*). Hand coloured engraving by François from an original drawing by Werner, pl. 1A from I. G. Saint-Hilaire's *Mammifères et Oiseaux* (in the *Atlas* to Bory de Saint-Vincent's *Expédition Scientifique de Morée*), 1832–36. Size of plate 18½″ × 11½″.

This is a very unusual representation of the wild cat. It looks less like the untamable savage creature we know it to be than an overfed domestic cat caught in the act of timidly climbing a tree. The stiff pose is due to the artist having had only a skin or a poorly mounted specimen as a model. Bory de Saint-Vincent, the leader of the French expedition to Morea in southern Greece, shot the specimen illustrated. Representations of the larger animals in French natural history publications of the early nineteenth century have formal and somewhat wooden poses with minimal background scenery. The animals are depicted with great attention to detail but are seldom imbued with life. Illustrations such as this were primarily adjuncts to scientific descriptions and were not intended to be appreciated as works of art with a separate existence.

In the text to this engraving Isidore Geoffroy Saint-Hilaire said there were minor differences between this form of the wild cat and that typical of other parts of Europe. In particular it had more marked rings around its tail. It was said to be very common on Morea and habitually rested for long periods in trees.

Numbat

Marsupial Anteater, *Myrmecobius fasciatus* (now Numbat, *Myrmecobius fasciatus*). Hand coloured lithograph by W. Dickes, pl. 27 from George R. Waterhouse's *Description of the new genus of mammiferous animals from Australia* (in *Transactions of the Zoological Society of London* Vol. 2), 1836. Size of plate 12½" × 10".

This curious animal, the size of a large ferret, lives in open wooded districts of south-western Australia, especially where dead eucalyptus branches are lying about. It obtains its food, principally termites, at or just under the surface and from under fallen branches, using its sticky, four-inch-long tongue.

George Waterhouse, who first brought this distinctively marked marsupial to the attention of the scientific world in 1836, tells us in the text to this illustration that the first example was found by a Lieutenant Dale of Liverpool while accompanying a party exploring the interior of the country at the Swan River Settlement about 90 miles north of the Swan River. Information he had received from Dale about this and another example make interesting reading. 'Two of these animals', said Dale, 'were seen within a few miles of each other; they were first observed on the ground, and on being pursued, both directed their flight to some hollow trees which were near. We succeeded in capturing one of them; the other was unfortunately burnt to death in our endeavour to dislodge it by fumigating the hollow tree in which it had taken refuge. The country in which they were found, abounded in decayed trees and ant-hills. The second individual, I am informed, was found in Van Diemen's Land [Tasmania]; and others, similar to it have been seen in the act of burrowing or digging at the roots of trees in search of insects. The favourite haunts are stated to be in those situations in which the Port Jackson willow abounds.' As no other specimen has ever been recorded from Tasmania it is likely that someone had misinformed Waterhouse.

Myrmecobius fasciatus

Giraffe

GIRAFFE, *Camelopardalis giraffa* (now Giraffe, *Giraffa camelopardalis*). Hand coloured engraving by W. Warwick after an original drawing by Captain Thomas Brown, pl. 52 from Part B of *The Edinburgh Journal of Natural History*, 1836–37. Size of plate 13½″ × 9″.

When this excellent engraving was published it was sufficient to call a giraffe a giraffe. Now as many as twelve different races are recognised, the visible differences between them, apart from size, being their dissimilar colours and colour patterns – although the differences are often subtle. Captain Brown would appear to have drawn the Nubian giraffe, distinguished by its white legs and broad, geometrical dark patches separated by thick white lines. This race, which occurs in the Sudan, was the first to be described.

The tallest animal in the world, the giraffe's statistics are impressive. Its height at the shoulder is 10–12 feet, at the top of the head 14–18 feet; its tongue is 7 inches long; and it weighs well over 2000 pounds. Both sexes have short horns covered with hair. A giraffe has a fair turn of speed, timed at up to 35 m.p.h. When galloping it swings the hind feet forwards and to the outside of the forefeet; both sets of legs move together, unlike those of a horse, which move diagonally.

The giraffe is a browser and the main advantage of its great height is to make available sources of food which other browsers cannot reach. But its height has the disadvantage of making it visible from a considerable distance; a giraffe cannot hide easily. So it falls prey to the lion, especially when drinking or when feeding at ground level. It is not defenceless, however, and can deliver a kick which may disable or kill even the King of Beasts.

Drawn by Captain Brown.

CAMELOPARDALIS GIRAFFA.
THE GIRAFFE.

Engraved by Wm Warwick.

Asiatic Elephant and African Elephant

INDIAN ELEPHANT, *Elephas indicus* (now Asiatic Elephant, *Elephas maximus*) (top), African Elephant, *Elephas africanus* (now African Elephant, *Loxodonta africana*) (bottom). Hand coloured engraving by S. Milne, pl. 39 from *The Edinburgh Journal of Natural History*, 1837. Size of plate 13½″ × 9″.

This plate is a mixture of fact and fable: the top figure is a tolerably accurate representation of the Asiatic elephant, the bottom little more than a caricature of the African elephant. The principal differences between the two species, though subtle, are well within the capacity of a competent artist to delineate. The African elephant, much the bigger animal, has considerably larger ears and the ridge of its back has a concave curve. It has three nails on each hind foot to the Asiatic elephant's four; and its trunk has two 'fingers' at its tip, the Asiatic elephant having only one. By at least some of these criteria the top figure represents an Asiatic elephant. The bottom figure, by almost any criterion, does not represent the African elephant.

As the distinguishing characteristics of the two animals were well known in 1837, when this picture was published, it is puzzling to see the African elephant portrayed here so inaccurately. But there may be a simple explanation: plagiarism. It was a common practice throughout the eighteenth century and well into the nineteenth for engravings to be copied without acknowledgment. This picture of the African elephant, so called, is almost certainly a copy or a near copy of one published earlier, possibly much earlier. Very similar pictures occur in several eighteenth-century publications. No elephant resembling this one has been at large anywhere outside an artist's imagination.

Maréchal Delt

ELEPHAS. ELEPHANTS.
1st Indian   E. Indicus.
2nd African _ Africanus Fem.

Engraved by S. Milne.

Greater Kudu

KOODOO, *Damalis (Strepsiceros) capensis* (now Greater Kudu, *Tragelaphus strepsiceros*). Hand coloured lithograph, pl. 42 from Vol. 1 of A. Smith's *Illustrations of the Zoology of South Africa*, 1838–50. Size of plate 11¾″ × 9¼″.

'When the southern parts of Africa were first colonised', says Andrew Smith in his monumental study of the fauna of South Africa, 'Koodoos were frequently discovered even in the vicinity of the locality where Cape Town now stands. The efficient weapons of the European hunters, however, soon diminished the number, and now specimens are rarely to be found within the Colony . . . The Koodoo is an animal naturally shy and timid, and on being disturbed in its retreats, immediately takes to flight . . . Its gait is elegant, its pace a moderately swift gallop, and while progressing it often springs over distances with great agility, and its bounds are frequently very expansive.'

This illustration shows two of the features distinguishing the male of the greater from the male of the lesser kudu: the white chevron between the eyes and the more developed, more widely divergent horns which spread in two to three open spirals. A fully grown greater kudu, one of the larger antelopes, stands five feet high at the shoulder and the horns themselves may be more than five feet long when measured along the spiral turns. The females of the greater kudu lack horns and are much smaller than the males. No antelope makes a louder sound than the deep bellow of this noble creature. Andrew Smith would not be surprised to know that the greater kudu, an easy target for a man with a gun, is no longer to be seen in the wild in the southern part of South Africa.

DAMALIS (Strepsiceros) CAPENSIS.
(Mammalia ___ Plate 42. Male)

Gemsbok

GEMSBOK, *Oryx capensis* (now *Oryx gazella*). Hand coloured lithograph by Frank Howard from an original drawing by Captain W. Cornwallis Harris, pl. 9 from Harris's *Portraits of the Game and Wild Animals of Southern Africa Delineated from Life in their Native Haunts*, 1840. Size of plate 21¼" × 14¼".

Captain Cornwallis Harris probably chose to represent the gemsbok in profile partly to show off the tuft of black hair at its throat. This feature, together with its black facial and flank markings, distinguishes it from other species of oryx. The sandy ground colour broken up by the black markings make this large antelope almost invisible in the African veldt.

Like most antelopes the gemsbok's horns are its crowning glory, measuring up to 44 inches in length and projecting straight upwards and backwards from the head, the longest and most impressive horns of all the oryx. Although shy by nature and a fast runner, it will turn and fight if pursued closely by a predator, and can use its horns with deadly effect. A pack of hounds is no match for it and it is believed to have killed lions with its well aimed rapier thrusts.

Gemsbok usually travel in herds of 30–40 head, but they are sometimes seen in hundreds. As they frequent arid regions they must be able to withstand long periods without water. They travel long distances to get at a water supply but, in times of drought, they supplement their diet of grasses with succulent wild fruits, such as melons and cucumbers.

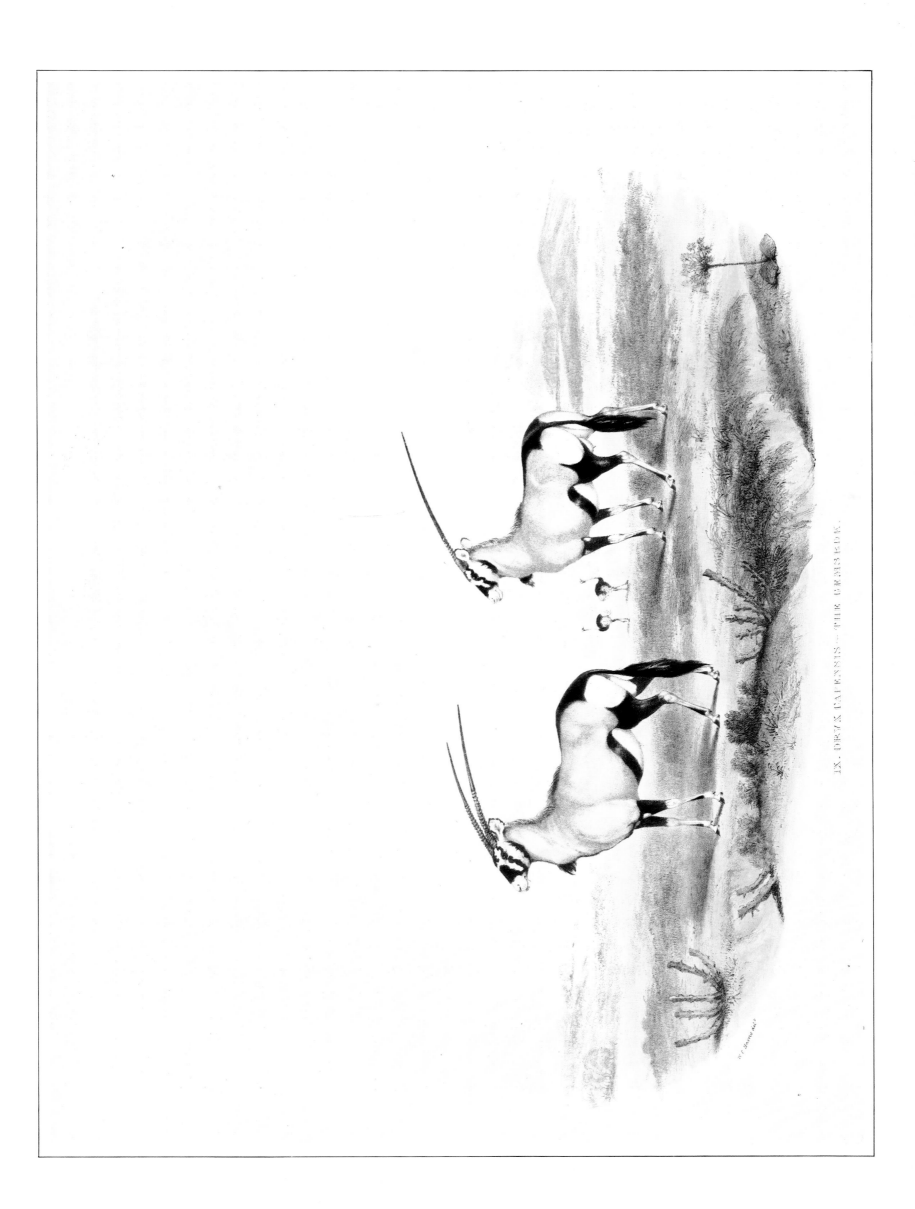

IX. ORYX CAPENSIS.—THE GEMSBOK.

African Buffalo

AFRICAN BUFFALO, *Bubalus caffer* (now African Buffalo, *Synceros caffer*). Hand coloured lithograph by Frank Howard from an original drawing by Captain W. Cornwallis Harris, pl. 13 from Harris's *Portraits of the Game and Wild Animals of Southern Africa Delineated from Life in their Native Haunts*, 1840. Size of plate 21¼″ × 14¼″.

Who can doubt that, for Captain Harris, the most important feature of this animal was its horns? They seem to dominate the entire composition, just as a fine pair of them may have dominated the wall over the Captain's own mantelpiece at home, for this is one of the most respected and most coveted of all game animals. More like an ox than a buffalo, it varies so much in size, shape, and colour that several different forms have been described, that portrayed in this lithograph being the distinctive Cape buffalo from open habitats in southern Africa. This form is much larger, heavier built, and blacker than the other well defined form, the dwarf forest buffalo from the forests of West and Central Africa. Neither form is found very far from water.

The horns of the Cape buffalo are very large, measuring up to a daunting 64 inches maximum width, and contribute significantly to the animal's total weight, which may exceed 1500 pounds. Normally of a peaceful temperament it can become very dangerous when wounded or cornered and many hunters have accused it of deliberate savagery – an accusation which may reasonably be levelled against the hunters themselves.

Apart from its human persecutors the African buffalo, in all its forms, has one principal enemy, the lion, which marks out cows or calves as they become separated from the herd. The crocodile will also prey on them when they are crossing rivers. Towards the close of the nineteenth century the African buffalo was decimated by outbreaks of rinderpest and in some districts has not regained its former population levels. Elsewhere, particularly in East Africa, it is more abundant now than formerly, one of Nature's success stories.

BOS BUBALUS (CAFFER).—THE AFRICAN BUFFALO.

Brown Bear

OURS BRUN, *Ursus arctos* (now Brown Bear, *Ursus arctos*). Hand coloured engraving by A. Dumenil from an original drawing by Werner, pl. 4 from I. G. Saint-Hilaire's *Mammifères* (in *Atlas, Zoologie* to A. Du Petit-Thouars's *Voyage autour du Monde sur . . . la Vénus*), 1840–64. Size of plate 16″ × 10¾″.

The text to this engraving says that the animal depicted was collected alive by members of the *Vénus* expedition. It had been eating a salmon when captured by the seashore at the southern extremity of the Kamchatka Peninsula, close to Petropavlovsk. When installed in the menagerie of the Jardin des Plantes at Paris in September 1837 it was reckoned to be about four years old. Werner made this drawing of it when it was still alive.

Formerly the brown bear was widely distributed over much of the northern hemisphere and used to be common in Europe, where now only a few isolated populations survive. It is still a familiar sight in North America but only in parts of Russia is it still plentiful in the wild. Many different subspecies of the brown bear have been described, including the Kodiak form from Alaska, which may weigh up to three-quarters of a ton, but it is now agreed that all represent variations within a single species. It is omnivorous, has few natural enemies and is solitary. Fortunately for its continued survival it also breeds more freely in captivity than any other kind of bear.

Peint par Werner.

Dirigé par Bouvenier.

Gravé par A. Dumenil.

Gide, Éditeur.

Imp.ᵉ de Bougeard.

OURS BRUN, *URSUS ARCTOS*, L.; Var. du Kamtschatka.

Slender-tailed Cloud Rat

PHLOEMYS DE CUMING, *Phloemys cumingi* (now Slender-tailed Cloud Rat, *Phloemys cumingi*). Hand coloured engraving by Annedouche from an original drawing by Werner, pl. 8 from the *Atlas* to J. F. T. Eydoux and L. F. A. Souleyet's *Zoologie* (in *Voyage autour du Monde . . . sur . . . la Bonite*), 1841–42. Size of plate 12¾″ × 9½″.

This is an early illustration of one of the largest rats in the world and is based on a specimen collected during the global voyage of the *Bonite* between 1836 and 1837, one of several voyages of discovery and exploration sent out by the French government during the first half of the nineteenth century. The head and body together measure about nineteen inches, to which should be added a tail length of about eleven or twelve inches, making the animal the size of a very large domestic cat. It has rough fur, paler underneath than above, and its feet are adapted to a tree-living existence.

The slender-tailed cloud rat is found only in mountainous districts on the island of Luzon in the Philippines where it was first collected in the late 1830s by an Englishman, Hugh Cuming, whence it was brought to England and described as new to science. Cuming spent four years in the Philippines, spending all his time collecting animals and plants. He was mainly interested in marine and non-marine molluscs, hundreds of those he collected proving to be new to science, but he brought many other previously unknown animals to the attention of scientists, who often named them after their discoverer. This rat, one of his more significant mammalian discoveries, is scarce throughout its range and may not be much better known now than it was in his day.

PHLŒOMYS DE CUMING, Waterhouse.

Werner del.

Arthur Bertrand Editeur
J. Pruvost imp.

Smithson. sc.

Arab Horse

ARABIAN HORSE (now Arab Horse, *Equus caballus*). Hand coloured lithograph from a drawing by W. Nicholson after a painting by W. Shiels, pl. 1 from Vol. 1 of D. Low's *The Breeds of the Domestic Animals of the British Islands*, 1842. Size of plate 17″ × 13″.

David Low has an interesting story to tell about the horse in this picture which, like all the animals portrayed in his excellent book, was originally the subject of a painting by William Shiels, a painter from Berwickshire. 'The figure in the Plate represents correctly the form of the genuine Arab', says Low. 'The horse here represented was taken in an attack by an Arab tribe on a party of the Royal Family of Persia, when journeying on a pilgrimage. The Arab chief who headed the attacking party was killed, and his charger, running into the Persian ranks, was taken. A ransom, enormous for so poor a tribe, was subsequently offered by the Arabs for their noble horse, but refused; and he was brought to England by Sir John M'Neill. He stands fourteen and a half hands high. He is gentle in the highest degree, and so thoroughly trained to that kind of exercise which the Arabs are careful to teach their horses, that he may be galloped around the narrowest circle. When his portrait was in the course of being painted, he was languid from the cold of the weather. It was wished to rouse him for a little, and the idea occurred of trying the effect of some tones of simple music. The sounds no sooner struck his ear than his whole frame was agitated; his heart throbbed so violently as to be seen beating; and so great was his excitement, that it was necessary instantly to stop the music. Some chord of feeling, it seems, had been struck: perchance he was reminded for a moment of his desert home, and of the friends from whom he had been so rudely severed.'

The Arab, often considered to be the principal ancestor of most breeds of light horse (but actually descended from a northern African type) is noted for its elegance and its intelligence. It is rightly held in great esteem by Bedouin horsemen but its small size has prevented it from achieving great popularity among western nations where it is not considered enough for a horse to be elegant and intelligent.

Plate I

THE ARABIAN.

Stallion, taken in a skirmish with an Arab Tribe, brought to England by Sir John McNeill, British Ambassador at the Court of Persia.

PROFESSOR LOW'S ILLUSTRATIONS OF THE BREEDS OF THE DOMESTIC ANIMALS.

Drawn on Stone & Printed by Fairland

Drawn by W. Nicholson, R.S.A. from a Painting by W. Shiels, R.S.A.

Hereford Cattle

HEREFORD BREED (now Hereford Cattle, *Bos taurus*). Hand coloured lithograph from a drawing by W. Nicholson after a painting by W. Shiels, pl. 17 from Vol. 1 of D. Low's *The Breeds of the Domestic Animals of the British Islands*, 1842. Size of plate 17″ × 13″.

This picture may puzzle some of those acquainted with today's breed of Hereford cattle. Many Herefords now lack horns, for instance, and also differ in other characteristics. Selective breeding has altered the breed considerably since William Shiels painted this picture, though the white face is still a Hereford hallmark. Even in Low's time, however, the breed was of long ancestry and mixed characters. His text is a historical document of interest both to cattle breeders and to those who merely gaze at cattle from over farm fences.

The cow in the foreground was the property of the Earl of Talbot and was descended from the stock of Benjamin Tomkins of King's Pyon in Herefordshire, a gentleman who influenced the characters of the breed profoundly. 'About the year 1769', says Low, 'the late Mr Benjamin Tomkins began a system of breeding, which ultimately exercised a great influence on the stock of this part of England. It appears that size, and adaptation to the dairy and the purposes of labour, were than the properties chiefly sought for by the breeders of Herefordshire. Mr Tomkins, when a young man, was in the employment of an individual, afterwards his father-in-law, and had the especial charge of the dairy. Two cows had been brought to this dairy, supposed to have been purchased at the fair of Kington, on the confines of Wales. Tomkins remarked the extraordinary tendency of these animals to become fat. On his marriage he acquired these two cows, and commenced breeding from them on his own account. The one with more of white, he called Pigeon, and the other, of a rich red colour, with a spotted face, he called Mottle; and it is remarkable that the marking of the two cows may be distinguished in their descendants at the present day.' Pigeon and Mottle will probably continue to have a visible impact on the progress of the breed for a long time to come.

Plate XVII.

THE HEREFORD BREED.

Cow, bred by the Right Honourable the Earl of Talbot; descended from the Stock of Mr Tonkins of Kingspion, Hereford.

PROFESSOR LOW'S ILLUSTRATIONS OF THE BREEDS OF THE DOMESTIC ANIMALS.

London, Published February 1842, by Longman, Brown, Green, & Longmans, Paternoster Row.

Drawn by Mr Nicholson, R.S.A. from ... Printing by W. Shaw R.S.A.

Lincoln Longwool Sheep

OLD LINCOLN BREED (now Lincoln Longwool Sheep, *Ovis aries*). Hand coloured lithograph from a drawing by W. Nicholson after a painting by W. Shiels, pl. 16 from Vol. 2 of D. Low's *The Breeds of the Domestic Animals of the British Islands*, 1842. Size of plate 17″ × 13″.

British breeds of sheep comprise longwools and shortwools. The Lincoln represents one of the longwool breeds, some other examples being the English Leicester, the Romney Marsh, the Cotswold, and the Wensleydale, the last being the only horned longwool. According to Low the extraordinary looking animal portrayed here came from a flock which had been maintained perfectly pure, retaining all the essential characters of the ancient race and presenting, perhaps, 'the only living example of the most remarkable breed of sheep which the British Islands have produced'.

Descendants of the original Lincoln Longwool have been much exported, especially to Argentina, so they are commonplace today. As the original reasons for the popularity of the breed may be unfamiliar, the following comments by Low are worth repeating. 'The Old Lincoln Sheep, of which the remnants only now exist, are destitute of horns, are of coarse form, have large limbs and hoofs, hollow flanks, and flat sides. Their long unctuous wool almost hangs to the ground, and they have a large tuft on the forehead. Their fleece weighs from 10 to 12 lb. and in the rams and fattened wethers, often greatly exceeds this weight. They are slow feeders, and consume much food, but are valued by the butchers for their tendency to produce internal fat.'

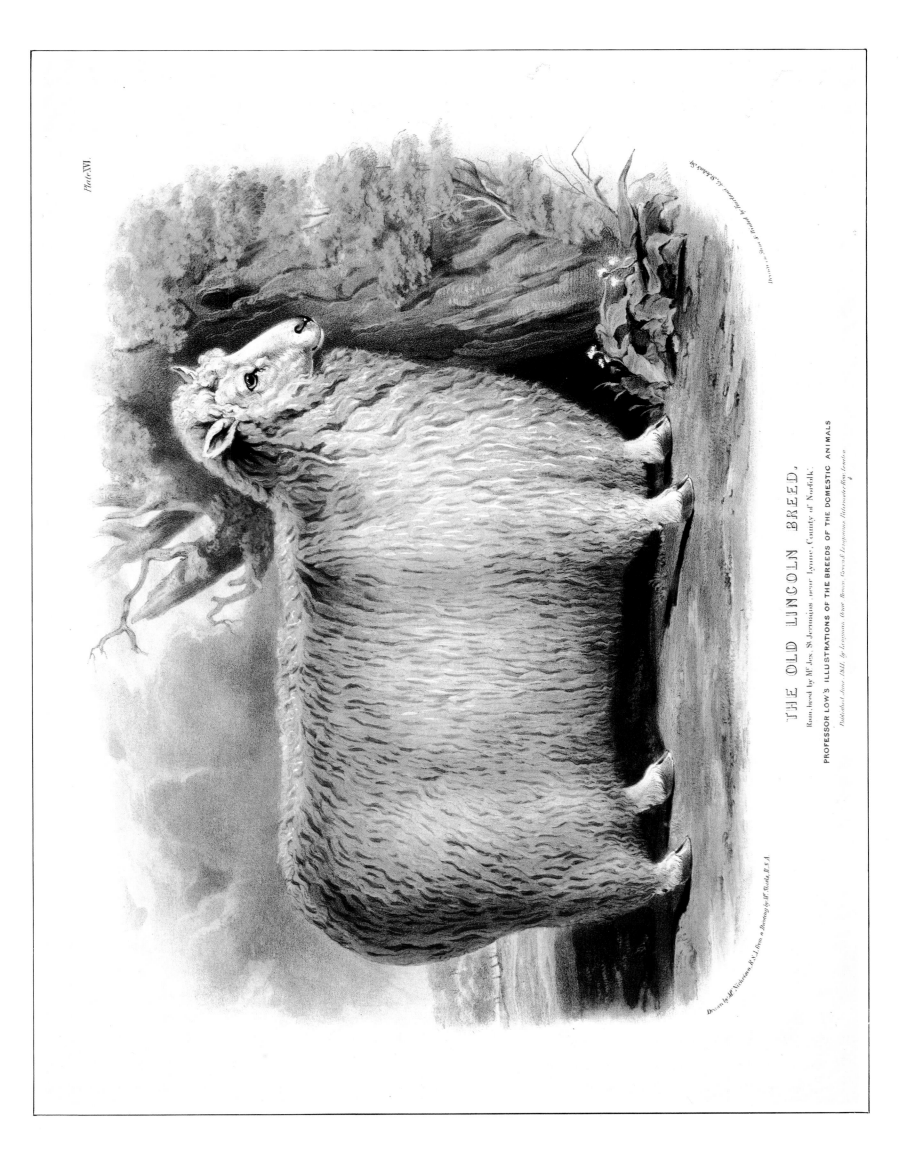

Plate XVI.

THE OLD LINCOLN BREED.

Ram, bred by Mr Jex, St Jermains, near Lynne, County of Norfolk.

PROFESSOR LOW'S ILLUSTRATIONS OF THE BREEDS OF THE DOMESTIC ANIMALS

Published June 1841, by Longman, Orme, Brown, Green & Longmans Paternoster Row London.

Drawn by Mr Nicholson, R.S.A. from a Painting by Mr Shiels, R.S.A.

Drawn on Stone & Printed by Day & Haghe, lith.

Hog-nosed Skunk

LONG-NOSED SKUNK, *Mephitis nasuta* (now Hog-nosed Skunk, *Conepatus mesoleucus*). Hand coloured lithograph by Charles Couzens, pl. 7 from L. Fraser's *Zoologia Typica*, 1845–49. Size of plate 14½" × 10½".

This lithograph from Louis Fraser's little-known *Zoologia Typica* makes the unfortunately-named hog-nosed skunk seem almost glamorous. Skunks are not popular mammals because we associate them with unpleasant smells (though most of us have never smelt one) and because they have an unmusical collective name. But these negative attributes should be measured against the attractiveness of their fur, which is usually glossy and strikingly marked in black and white.

There are seven different types of hog-nosed skunk in the southern United States and South America, each characterised by the pig-like shape of its nose. Measuring about two and a half feet from nose to tail tip the one illustrated here is slow moving and nocturnal in its habits. It uses its snout to root about in the soil for grubs and insects, but it will also eat small mammals and snakes. Living in wooded and open land, sometimes occupying burrows abandoned by other animals, it produces a litter of two to five young. It ranges from the southern United States to Nicaragua and has been hunted occasionally for its fur which, contrary to the impression given by this illustration, is not soft but coarse.

MEPHITIS NASUTA.

Koala

KOALA, *Phascolarctos cinereus*. Hand coloured lithograph by J. Gould and H. C. Richter, pl. 14 from Vol. 1 of J. Gould's *The Mammals of Australia*, 1845–63. Size of plate 21½″ × 14½″.

When you see a koala curled up in the fork of a swaying sapling with a youngster clinging to its back you wonder how it got there and how it stays there. As its hands and feet are specialised climbing organs it has no difficulty installing itself in such a place; and because each of its limbs has two clawed fingers which oppose the other three and provide it with a very firm grip it is not easily dislodged. John Gould often had a vivid demonstration of the koala's reluctance to let go when he was collecting materials for his book about Australian mammals in the late 1830s. In those days the acceptable way to collect mammals, even lethargic and inoffensive ones, was to shoot them, and Gould seems to have considered it necessary to shoot many koalas. 'Those that fell to my gun', he says, 'were most tenacious of life, clinging to the branches until the last spark had fled.' Not surprisingly these endearing creatures suffered an alarming decline in numbers until protective measures were taken, millions having been killed for their fur; epidemic diseases, fires and forest clearances have also taken their toll.

Unlike most mammals the koala feeds almost exclusively upon the leaves of eucalyptus trees, and it requires two or three pounds of such leaves each day to remain healthy. As the leaves must also be of a certain age and must come from only certain species of eucalyptus grown in the right kind of soil it is difficult to feed them in captivity. Under normal conditions eucalyptus leaves provide sufficient water for the koala to disdain drinking.

PHASCOLARCTOS CINEREUS.

J. Gould and H.C. Richter del. et lith.   Hullmandel & Walton, Imp.

Thylacine

THYLACINUS, *Thylacinus cynocephalus* (now Thylacine, *Thylacinus cynocephalus*). Hand coloured lithograph by H. C. Richter, pl. 54 from Vol. 1 of J. Gould's *The Mammals of Australia*, 1845–63. Size of plate 21½″ × 14½″.

The thylacine is an enigmatic creature. It was thought to be related to the oppossums when first described in 1808; the seventeen dark stripes on its back earned it the name Tasmanian tiger; and its dog-like shape, very long incisors and habit of running on its toes earned it the alternative name Tasmanian wolf. Once widespread over much of New Guinea and Australia it survived into modern times only in Tasmania. A wild thylacine was captured in Tasmania in 1933 and survived in captivity until 1936. It has not been sighted positively since then. There is slender evidence to show that one may have entered and escaped from a trap on the west coast in 1961; and a later photograph provides further, equally slender proof that it may not be extinct.

Largest of the carnivorous marsupials, the thylacine fed mostly on kangaroos and wallabies, but the early colonists claimed that it preyed upon their sheep and poultry and waged ceaseless war on it. In the text to this plate John Gould described the early effect of that war: 'The destruction it deals around has, as a matter of course, called forth the enmity of the settler, and hence in all cultivated districts the animal is nearly extirpated; on the other hand, so much of Tasmania still remains in a state of nature, and so much of its forest land yet uncleared, that an abundance of covert still remains in which the animal is secure from the attacks of man; many years must therefore elapse before it can become entirely extinct.' Alas, the many years seem to have elapsed. The only thylacines in existence are probably those on display in museums.

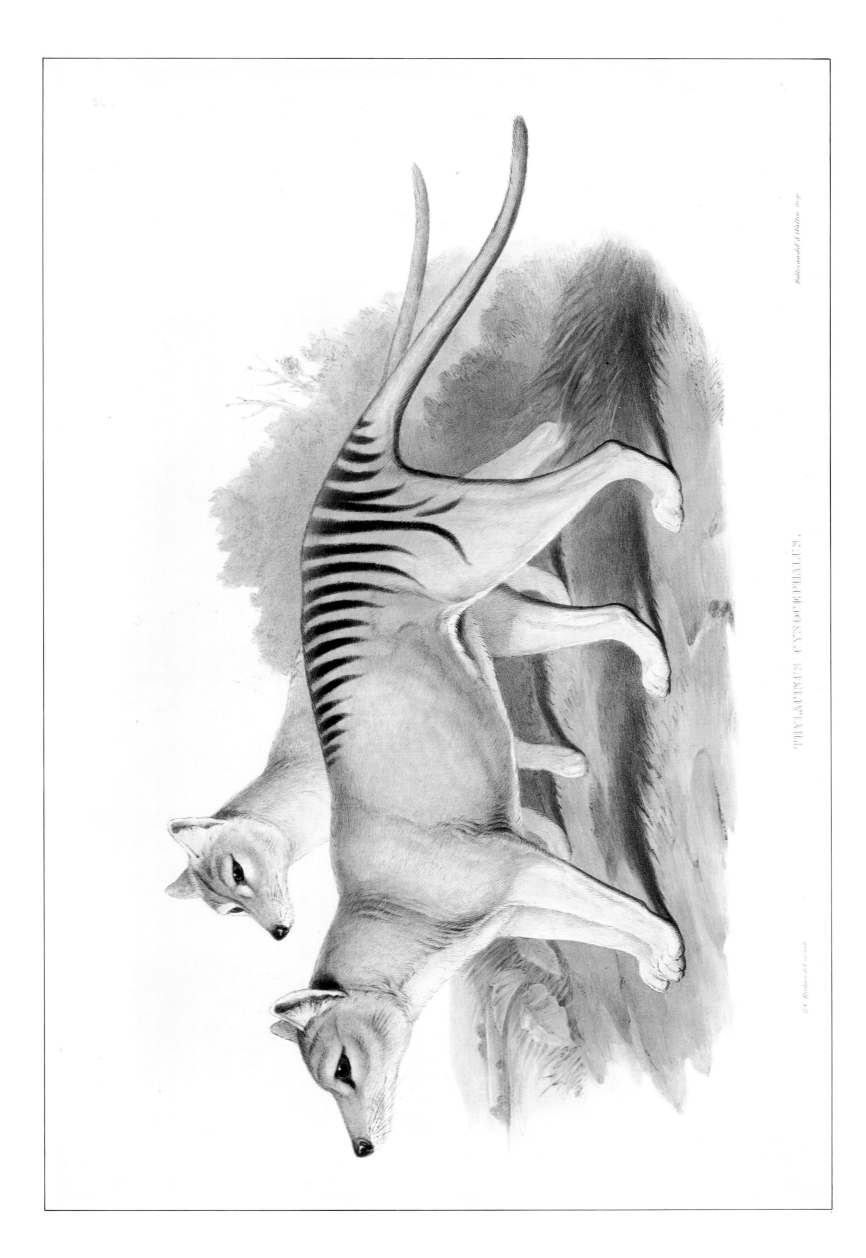

THYLACINUS CYNOCEPHALUS.

Wallaroo

BLACK WALLAROO, *Osphranter robustus* (now Wallaroo, *Macropus robustus*). Hand coloured lithograph by H. C. Richter, pl. 11 from Vol. 2 of J. Gould's *The Mammals of Australia*, 1845–63. Size of plate 21½″ × 14½″.

Participants in Captain Cook's first voyage of exploration to the Pacific may have seen and captured this marsupial in 1770 near the Endeavour River on the east coast of Australia. But it was not until after John Gould returned to England in 1840, with specimens he had obtained near the Liverpool Range in New South Wales, that it was described as a species new to science.

Years later Gould expressed surprise that it was not better known. 'I have in vain requested my numerous friends and correspondents to procure and transmit examples of this large and truly fine animal', he said in the text to this lithograph. 'I believe I was the first scientific man who visited the locality in which it dwells as well as the first who made it known to science; and I may ask, is it not surprising that during the interval of fifteen years which has elapsed since the account of this species was published in my "Monograph of the Kangaroos", no examples besides those I myself brought home should have been procured, and that no attempts to secure living examples of so conspicuous an animal should have been attempted? Indeed, were it not for my visit to its native haunts, it might have remained unknown to us even to the present time. This is the more to be wondered at, since the animal is found within the colony of New South Wales. Surely the exterminating hand of civilized man, so fatal to the animal productions of a new country, cannot have dealt out destruction so unsparingly as to have destroyed the entire race.'

Fortunately the 'exterminating hand' did not eliminate the seven foot long wallaroo, which is still widely distributed in eastern Australia, mainly in mountainous regions. Occasionally it will shelter in caves and it has been known to go without water for two or three months. Evidently it is a survivor.

OSPHRANTER ROBUSTUS, Gould.

Grey-headed Flying Fox

GREY-HEADED VAMPIRE, *Pteropus poliocephalus* (now Grey-headed Flying Fox). Hand coloured lithograph by J. Gould and H. C. Richter, pl. 28 from Vol. 3 of J. Gould's *The Mammals of Australia*, 1845–63. Size of plate 21½″ × 14½″.

Flying foxes are widespread on island groups in the Indian and Pacific Oceans and Australia is home to several species. The larger species have wingspans of up to five feet. Unlike many of the smaller bats, which navigate by echo-location, these giants of the bat world have large, functional eyes (they are larger than shown on the right-hand animal in this picture). They differ in other ways: their ears are smooth like those of non-flying mammals; and their noses lack the peculiar processes characteristic of many insect-eating bats. Gould's picture accurately represents the way flying foxes suspend themselves upside down. They feed on soft fruit and may roost in large groups. Many species are endangered because they are easily shot, may be hunted for food and are adversely affected by the destruction of forest habitats.

The grey-headed flying fox comes from eastern Australia where it is still common. It is victimised by fruit growers, who consider it threatens their livelihood, though it does not normally eat cultivated fruit unless its natural food is scarce.

Eastern Chipmunk

CHIPPING SQUIRREL, HACKEE, *Tamias lysteri* (now Eastern Chipmunk, *Tamias striatus*). Hand coloured lithograph from an original drawing by J. J. Audubon, pl. 8 from *Atlas*, Vol. 1 of J. J. Audubon and J. Bachman's *The Viviparous Quadrupeds of North America*, 1846–54. Size of plate 27¼″ × 20¾″.

Following the success of his monumental book *The Birds of America*, John James Audubon conceived the idea of writing and illustrating a similar book about the mammals of North America. The Revd John Bachman of Charleston, South Carolina, offered to help him with the writing. A careful and scientific observer of animal life, Bachman became co-author of *Viviparous Quadrupeds of North America* and spent a dozen years researching and writing. Members of Audubon's immediate family also provided much help, his son John Woodhouse Audubon contributing drawings which were lithographed and included in the book.

A caption at the foot of this lithograph says 'Male, female and young first autumn.' The young, presumably, are the skittish ones on the tree trunk. Five black and four pale stripes characterise the eastern chipmunk. A forest dweller in the eastern United States, it digs its own burrow and constructs therein a nest of dry plant material. It was known to Bachman as the 'Chipping Squirrel' because, as he remarked, 'its chucking resembles the chip, chip, chip, of a young chicken'. He wrote of its 'chops distended' by nuts and berries, in which condition Audubon has depicted the creature at bottom right. There are many different kinds of chipmunk, all but one of them confined to North America.

PLATE VIII.

Drawn from Nature by J.J. Audubon F.R.S.Fl.S.

Lith. Printed & Col.d by J.T.Bowen, Philad.a

TAMIAS LYSTERI, RAY.
CHIPPING SQUIRREL. HACKEE &c.
Natural Size

MALE, FEMALE AND YOUNG FIRST AUTUMN.

Long-tailed Weasel

BRIDLED WEASEL, *Putorius frenata* (now Long-tailed Weasel, *Mustela frenata*). Hand coloured lithograph from a drawing by J. J. Audubon, pl. 60 from *Atlas*, Vol. 2 of J. J. Audubon and J. Bachman's *The Viviparous Quadrupeds of North America*, 1846–54. Size of plate 27¼″ × 20¾″.

In spite of the enormous efforts put into the production of *The Viviparous Quadrupeds of North America* by John James Audubon, the Revd John Bachman and their respective families, factual and artistic mistakes were inevitable. Even some of the larger mammals were poorly known in their day. But the smaller ones were especially puzzling; specimens of certain species could be difficult to come by, the life histories of most were unknown – and there were so many of them. The treatment of the weasels, for instance, shows an incomplete understanding of their sexual size differences and the different appearances resulting from the seasonal moult, but this is hardly surprising. Bearing in mind the vastness of the North American wilderness, the problems of travel and the imperfect state of contemporary biological knowledge (to say nothing of the difficulty of acquiring that knowledge far from centres of learning) it is remarkable that the Audubons and the Bachmans did not make many more mistakes.

The long-tailed weasel is very variable in appearance and several subspecies occur throughout North and Central America. Northern subspecies are white in winter, other subspecies only a lighter shade of brown than in summer. The tip of the tail is black all year round. This illustration, a lively interpretation of the animal's appearance, has a curious subsidiary feature; the upper surface of the right-hand tree stump mirrors the attitude of the animal standing on it. Whether this effect was fortuitous or intentional we may never know, but it is easy to imagine Audubon smiling over it.

No. 12.

PLATE LX.

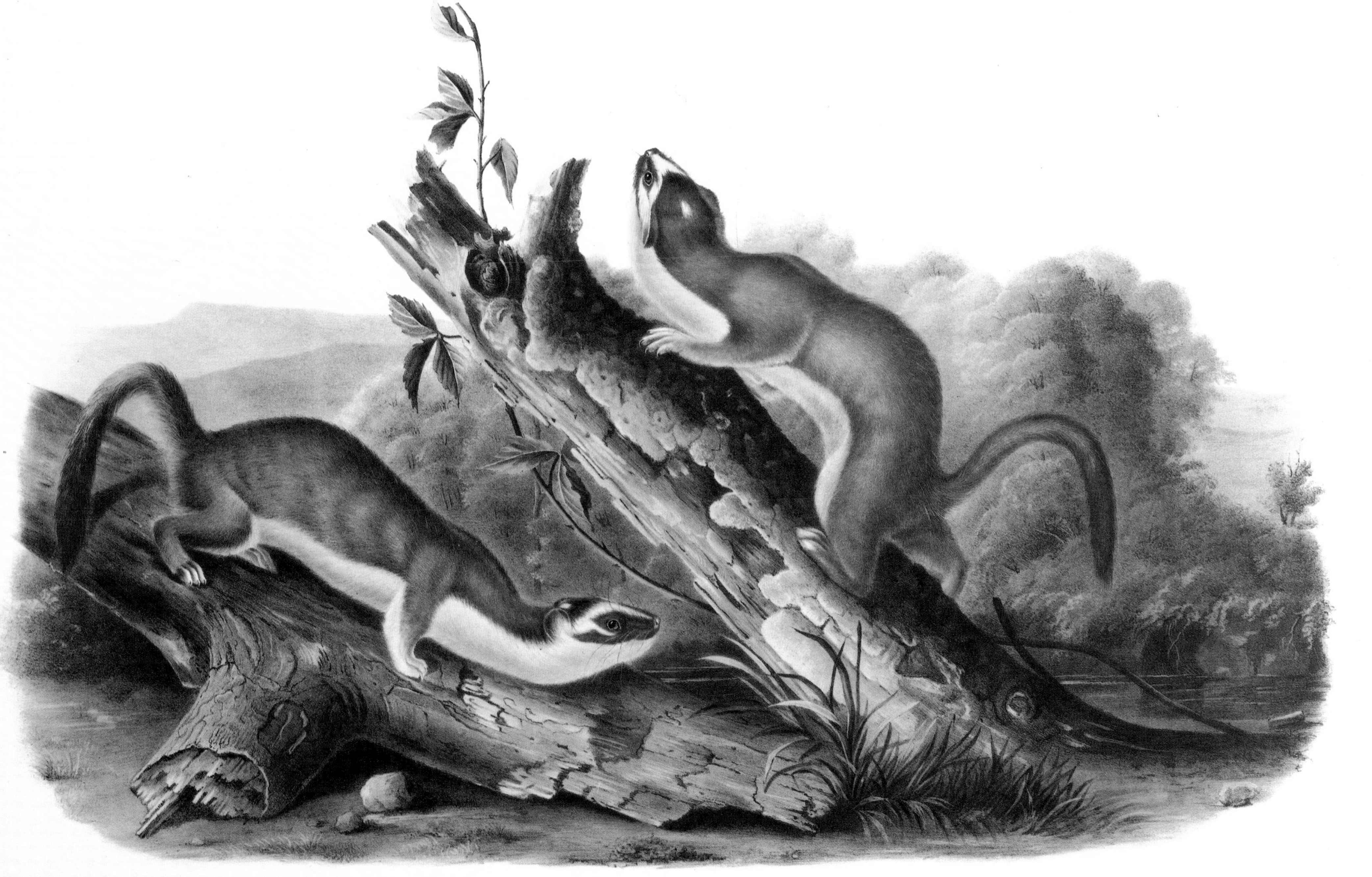

Drawn from Nature by J. J. Audubon F.R.S F.L.S.

PUTORIUS FRENATA, LICHT.

BRIDLED WEASEL.

MALES.

Natural Size.

Northern Flying Squirrel

SEVERN RIVER FLYING SQUIRREL, *Pteromys sabrinus* (top), Rocky Mountain Flying Squirrel, *Pteromys alpinus* (bottom), (both now Northern Flying Squirrel, *Glaucomys sabrinus*). Hand coloured lithograph from an original drawing by J. J. Audubon, pl. 143 from *Atlas*, Vol. 3 of J. J. Audubon and J. Bachman's *The Viviparous Quadrupeds of North America*, 1846–54. Size of plate 27¼″ × 20¾″.

John James Audubon and the Revd John Bachman considered the two animals shown in this lithograph to be representatives of two different species, but each is a form of the northern flying squirrel, a common inhabitant of evergreen forests in Canada and the western United States. Large eyes give it the sharp vision required to undertake nocturnal flights safely. The upper figure shows how, in flight, it spreads the loose folds of fur-covered skin which extend from each side of its body and between its fore and hind limbs. When the legs are fully extended the stretched skin provides sufficient air resistance to enable it to glide downwards for a distance of well over 200 feet. The figure also shows how the tail is flattened out in flight, thus helping to control the direction in which the animal is travelling and acting as a brake. As soon as the animal lands on a tree trunk it scuttles around to the opposite side and so eludes any predators that may have followed its aerial journey.

Very agile and sure-footed, the northern flying squirrel usually lives in hollow trees in winter and builds an outside nest in summer. There is only one other flying squirrel in the United States, but many more occur in tropical and sub-tropical parts of the world. One of them, from Borneo, is a mere three and a half inches long; some others are up to three feet long.

PLATE CXLIII.

Fig 1.

Fig 2.

Drawn from Nature by J.W. Audubon

Fig 1. **PTEROMYS SABRINUS**, PENNANT | Fig 2. **PTEROMYS ALPINUS**, RICH.

SEVERN RIVER FLYING SQUIRREL.   ROCKY MOUNTAIN FLYING SQUIRREL.

Lith.d Printed & Col.d by J.T. Bowen, Phila.d 1848.

Orang Utan

OURANG OUTAN OR PONGO (now Orang Utan, *Pongo pygmaeus*). Hand coloured lithograph by W. Wing, pl. 1 from J. E. Gray's *Vertebrata* (in A. Adams' *The Zoology of the Voyage of H. M. S. Samarang; under the Command of Captain Sir E. Belcher*), 1848–50. Size of plate 10″ × 8″.

This picture reveals much more about mid-nineteenth-century attitudes and beliefs than it does about the physical appearance of the orang utan (a Malay expression meaning 'man of the forest'). Before 1869, when Alfred Russell Wallace published his personal observations of the animal sometimes called 'the wild man of Borneo', the man-like apes had been represented in popular literature as creatures with distinctly human attributes. The orang utan, then known mostly from hearsay evidence, had usually been illustrated in books standing or sitting; often, as here, it had been given a stick to hold. The idea of 'wild men' existing in remote, thickly forested places had been circulating in Europe for three or four centuries and the orang utan was seized upon eagerly as an embodiment of that idea. This picture, published in a scientific report, shows that the idea was acceptable even to professional natural historians such as the author of the report, John Edward Gray, then Keeper of Zoology at the British Museum.

The orang utan is confined in the wild to the islands of Borneo and Sumatra. Comparable in weight to an average human male, it is never more than four and a half feet tall, though it may have an arm spread of seven and a half feet. Primarily a tree dweller, it swings with slow and graceful movements from branch to branch, apparently testing the branches before trusting them with its weight. On the ground, however, it moves around awkwardly on all fours, as uncomfortable as a fish out of water. Unlike the other great apes, it is solitary by nature. The continued destruction of suitable habitats has reduced its numbers drastically but it exists in large numbers in zoos and breeds regularly in captivity.

OURANG OUTAN or PONGO.

Simia satyrus.

Eland

IMPOPHOO OR ELAND, *Oreas cauna* (now Eland, *Tragelaphus oryx*). Hand coloured lithograph by B. Waterhouse Hawkins, pl. 27 from Vol. 2 of J. E. Gray's *Gleanings from the Knowsley Menagerie and Aviary at Knowsley Hall,* 1850. Size of plate 22″ × 15″.

This massive antelope, measuring almost six feet at the shoulder and weighing up to 2000 pounds, must have been impressive when it was brought to Knowsley Hall near Liverpool. Lord Stanley had spent much money on his collection of exotic mammals and birds by the time this lithograph was published in 1850; a year later his menagerie contained 345 mammals belonging to 94 species. He employed agents throughout the world and financed expeditions to Africa, Central America and elsewhere in his search for rare and unusual species. Transporting a large and powerful animal such as this by sea from South Africa to England would have been no easy matter in those days and the earl must have been relieved to see it installed safely among his other living treasures.

Although rather more ox-like in appearance than this lithograph suggests, the eland does have a certain gracefulness about it and is surprisingly agile, jumping more than its own height with ease. It is timid and easily tamed, occasionally being used as a draught animal. As it also makes excellent eating and is more easily fattened than any other African antelope attempts have been made to domesticate it as though it were a species of cattle, with some success.

Like many antelopes its horns are distinctive. They are massive, about two and a half feet long (the record is 43½ inches), slightly diverging, and have a tight spiral towards the base. Of the several recognised forms of this antelope the one illustrated here is characterised by the absence of stripes in the adult. Other forms have vertical white stripes.

Guanaco

GUANACO, [*Lama huanaca*] (now Guanaco, *Lama guanicoe*). Hand coloured lithograph by B. Waterhouse Hawkins, pl. 50 from Vol. 2 of J. E. Gray's *Gleanings from the Knowsley Menagerie and Aviary at Knowsley Hall,* 1850. Size of plate 22″ × 15″.

The guanaco, an engaging and attractive animal with a well developed sense of curiosity, must have been a welcome addition to the Earl of Derby's menagerie at Knowsley Hall. Measuring about five feet to the top of its head, it is the tallest mammal native to South America. The guanaco is in the same family as the Old World camels although its ears are long and mobile and it lacks a hump. It moves like a camel but except for its long neck it is more like a sheep; the male even bleats like a sheep. It is found along the west coast from Peru southwards to Tierra del Fuego and may ascend as high as 13,000 feet in the rainy season to wander the treeless plains and passes of the Andes.

Guanacos congregate in small herds comprising a male, four to ten females and young ones of various ages; young males, on the other hand, will form themselves into herds of up to fifty strong. It is often said that the llama, *Lama glama*, is a domesticated form of the guanaco, but this ancestry may be disputed because there are striking differences between the behaviour of the two animals.

DRAWN from the LIVING ANIMALS at KNOWSLEY by B. WATERHOUSE HAWKINS. — Lithog June 1866

Hullmandel & Walton Lithographers

THE IMPOPHOO OR ELAND-BOSELAPHUS OREAS

DRAWN from the Living Animals at Knowsley October 1844 by B.W.Hawkins

Burchell's Zebra

BURCHELL'S ZEBRA, *Asinus burchellii* (now *Equus burchelli burchelli*). Hand coloured lithograph by B. Waterhouse Hawkins, pl. 55 from Vol. 2 of J. E. Gray's *Gleanings from the Knowsley Menagerie and Aviary at Knowsley Hall*, 1850. Size of plate 22″ × 15″.

This is not merely a charming and delicately drawn picture; it is also an invaluable scientific record, for the animal pictured here is extinct. John Edward Gray, an eminent zoologist at the British Museum and author of the book containing this lithograph, named and described Burchell's zebra in 1824 when it roamed the wilds of the Bechuanaland and Orange Free State territories of South Africa.

The familiar animals with bold black and white stripes on their hind legs, now occupying territories farther north in Africa, are often named Burchell's zebra but they represent different forms (named after their various discoverers). It seems as though the striping of zebras becomes more vivid and more detailed the farther north they occur, but that observation will not help to bring back the true Burchell's zebra; so this picture provides important evidence of the appearance of an animal future generations will never see. It is melancholy to reflect on the probable causes of the demise of so large and distinctive an animal so soon after William John Burchell brought it to the attention of the scientific world. Fortunately its near cousins are still plentiful both in the wild and in captivity.

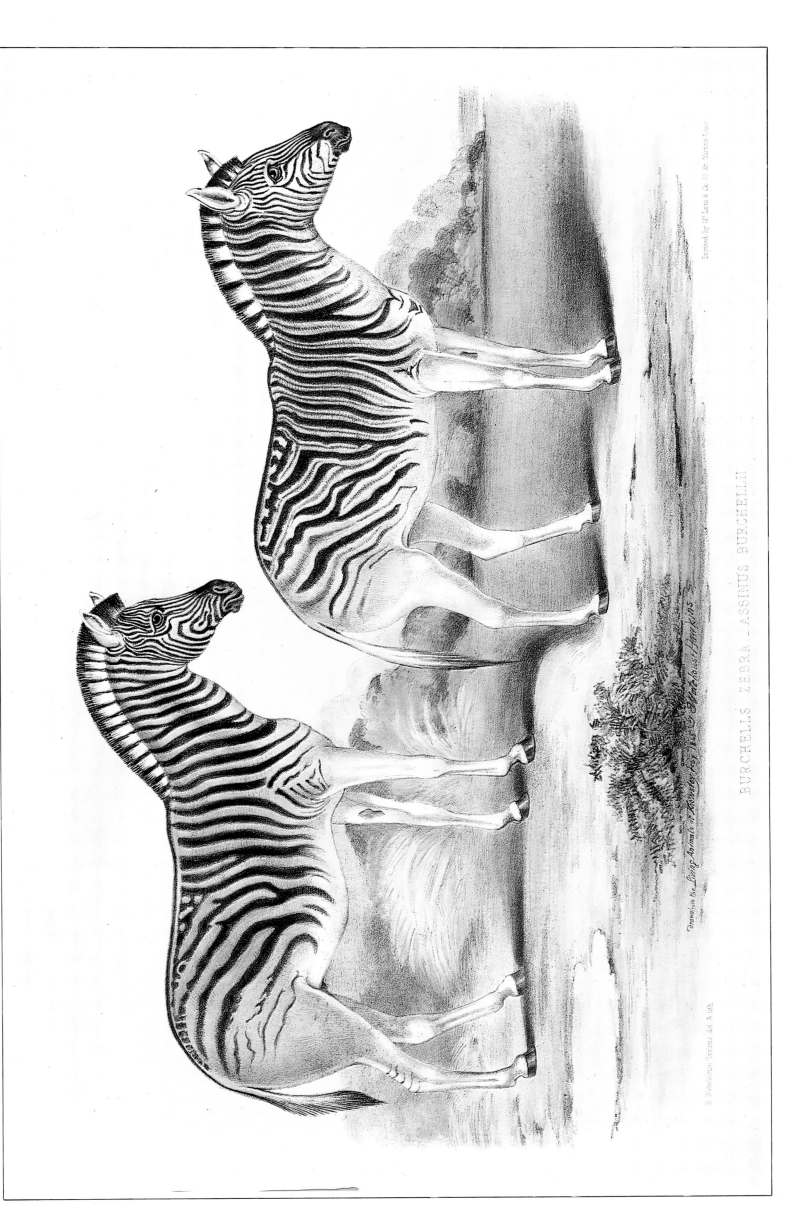

Drawn from the Living Animals at Knowsley 1832 1835 & by Waterhouse Hawkins.

Printed by Mr Laws & Co 76 St Martins Lane

B.W.Woodhouse Pardma Litho Studio

BURCHELL'S ZEBRA _ ASSINUS BURCHELLII

Gorilla

GORILLA, *Troglodytes gorilla* (now *Gorilla gorilla*). Hand coloured lithograph by Joseph Wolf, pl. 44 from Richard Owen's *Contributions to the natural history of the anthropoid apes* (in Vol. 5 of the *Transactions of the Zoological Society of London*, No. 8), 1865. Size of plate 12½″ × 10″.

There was only one recognised race of the largest living primate when Joseph Wolf produced this group portrait representing the lowland gorilla, an inhabitant of rain forests in west Central Africa. This form is distinguished by the silvery grey coat developed by the adult male. In 1901, however, a black, long-haired race was discovered on the Congo border, living in forests high up in the mountains. This race, now known as the mountain gorilla, may attain a height of six and a half feet and a weight of more than 500 pounds. The lowland gorilla, although smaller and lighter, is still a formidable creature.

This is one of two lithographs by Wolf which illustrated an article published in 1865 by the famous palaeontologist Richard Owen. Before that date the gorilla had been an almost legendary creature, and proof of its existence in darkest Africa was based mostly on travellers' tales. It was fashionable then to regard the gorilla as a bloodthirsty monster of hideous aspect with no redeeming features. Wolf's tender, even sentimental interpretation of it marked a new departure in our understanding of this gentle giant.

The gorilla is a vegetarian, notwithstanding its intimidating canine teeth. For most of the day it wanders about as part of a family group, nonchalantly munching succulent shoots and other forest produce, and sleeping at night on specially prepared beds of twigs and leaves. Apart from humans a fully grown gorilla has no natural enemies among predatory animals, does not kill except in self defence, and is usually content merely to scare off intruders with a show of noisy bravado. Wolf's picture has a remarkably modern look and must have annoyed those of his contemporaries who wanted to promote the idea of the gorilla as the embodiment of bestiality.

Maned Wolf

Canis jubatus (now Maned Wolf, *Chrysocyon brachyurus*). Hand coloured lithograph, pl. 21 from C. H. C. Burmeister's *Erlauterungen zur Fauna Brasiliens*, 1856. Size of plate 17½" × 12".

The maned wolf comes from northern Argentina, Paraguay and southern Brazil and is the largest member of the dog family in the southern hemisphere. It differs from the true wolves, all from the northern hemisphere, in both appearance and habits. In some ways it looks like a long-legged fox, a resemblance made the more striking by its pointed muzzle and bushy, white-tipped tail. The fur is long and soft, orange-red above the white below. What is not clearly seen in this picture is the mane of slightly longer fur on the neck, but this feature is revealed only when the animal is excited.

Its long legs help it to see over the top of the long vegetation covering the savanna and grasslands through which it roams in search of its food. It pursues wild deer, rats, birds, reptiles and other small animals, usually at night. On occasion it will also eat insects, snails, fruit and sugar cane. It will mate with the domestic dog and the resulting mongrels are said to make good hunting animals. The maned wolf, protected by law in several parts of its range, is exhibited in many of the larger zoos and breeds regularly in captivity.

Canis pictatus.

Mule Deer

BLACK-TAILED DEER, *Cervus lewisii* (now Mule Deer, *Odocoileus hemionus*). Hand coloured engraving from an original drawing by T. R. Peale, pl. 11 from the *Atlas* to J. Cassin's *Mammalogy and Ornithology* (in *United States Exploring Expedition . . . Under the Command of C. Wilkes*), 1858. Size of plate 16½″ × 11″.

Between 1838 and 1842 the United States Exploring Expedition investigated remote and little-known parts of the globe and did not ignore the natural history of the United States itself. This engraving, from an original drawing by Titian Rembrandt Peale, a naturalist–artist attached to the expedition, represents a mammal which occurs from southern Alaska to northern Mexico. Standing about three feet high at the shoulder, the mule deer had been described in 1807 in the *Journal* of the explorers Lewis and Clarke. It was well known by the time the Exploring Expedition report was published, but Peale had made some useful notes about it which were included therein. 'The Black-tailed Deer never carries its tail erect when running', he said. 'When on the prairies, in long grass, it has a habit which is somewhat peculiar – that of frequently springing up to a considerable height to get sight of its pursuers.'

There have been many advances in our knowledge of this deer since Peale observed it and several races of it have been described. Undoubtedly, too, it has been illustrated more accurately since this engraving of his drawing was published, but few illustrations published later are more appealing than his. Less a scientist than an artist, it was natural for Peale to make an animal portrait more than a dry factual record. By glamourising his subject he took it out of the realm of science and into that of art – which is why it continues to be worth looking at.

Cervus   Lewisii .   Peale.

Pale–throated Sloth

Yellow-throated Sloth, *Bradypus gularis* (now presumably Pale-throated Sloth, *Bradypus tridactylus*). Colour printed engraving, pl. 47 from M. H. H. T.'s *The Instructive Picture Book, Lessons from the Geographical Distribution of Animals*, 1860. Size of plate 10″ × 6¾″.

There are two groups of sloths, those with two claws on each fore limb and those with three on each fore limb (all sloths have three-clawed hind limbs). The pale-throated sloth, the creature supposedly portrayed here, belongs to the latter group and is found in the northern half of South America. Its specialised diet makes it almost impossible to keep in captivity, and as it seems to spend most of its life asleep it is difficult for us to get to know it well. Thus many fanciful notions have accrued around it. One early traveller said it lived on ants and another said it survived on air alone – although those who have observed it, if only briefly, know that it eats leaves. It has been considered incapable of covering more than fifty paces in a day – but some of those who have studied it in the wild have occasionally seen it move rapidly through the branches of forest trees. Those who have kept three-toed sloths as pets know that they are trusting, gentle and fascinating to study, even though they may require at least fifteen hours sleep a day.

This engraving dates from mid-Victorian times when little was known about the habits of sloths and their appearance in life was largely conjectural. But the creatures shown here look more like lively, black-faced nuns playing hide-and-seek in a tree than the shaggy-coated indolent creatures we know them to be. The artist was unable to resist the tendency to turn a little-known animal into a caricature of a familiar kind of human being. This was a common tendency among early animal artists, but it is remarkable to see such a blatant example served up for public consumption in the middle of the nineteenth century.

Red Howler

HOWLING MONKEY, *Mycetus ursinus* (now Red Howler, *Alouatta seniculus*). Hand coloured engraving, pl. 50 from M. H. H. T.'s *The Instructive Picture Book, Lessons from the Geographical Distribution of Animals*, 1860. Size of plate 10″ × 7″.

Although this engraving was intended to represent the red howler – an intention singularly unsuccessful in its execution – its principal, though unstated, purpose was to illustrate a story from the Bible. *The Instructive Picture Book* was one of many Victorian publications which tried to popularise natural history while attempting to put across religious messages. Often the text or the illustrations, sometimes both, would 'point a moral'. In this instance the very red apple in the very human hand of the squatting figure leaves us in no doubt that we are looking at Eve offering the fruit to Adam.

The red howler, an improbable actor in the Adam and Eve story, is one of the largest and noisiest of the New World monkeys. The engraving correctly represents the prehensile nature of the long tail – used almost as though it were an extra limb – but fails utterly to give a correct idea of any other part of the creature. No one who has seen a red howler squatting in a tree and has listened to it howling at the top of its voice would ever confuse it with the benign-looking creatures shown here. Evidently the artist did not work from living models. Like many Victorian popularisers of natural history he was guilty of plagiarism. The left-hand figure in this picture is based on a figure published in 1812 in a book describing and illustrating the zoological discoveries of the great German explorer/naturalist, Alexander von Humboldt. In Humboldt's original version the monkey's right hand is empty while its left hand grasps a pod-like vegetable or fruit. In most other respects the two figures are similar. For the right-hand figure the artist who produced the illustrations for *The Instructive Picture Book* seems to have used his own well-developed imagination entirely. Just possibly Adam may have looked like this – but never the red howler!

The coloration of the red howler may or may not resemble that of the engraving, for in captivity its coat may change colour after contact with water, red turning to orange and orange to yellow. If this kind of change is repeated in the wild, as is probable, it would explain why there has been disagreement among observers about its coloration.

Chimpanzee

CHIMPANZEE, *Troglodytes niger* (now *Pan troglodytes*). Hand coloured lithograph by J. Wolf, pl. 1 from *Zoological Sketches, First Series* (edited by D. W. Mitchell and P. L. Sclater) 1861. Size of plate 13¼″ × 9″.

During the nineteenth century there was little hope of a chimpanzee surviving for long in England or other European countries. The one shown here, for instance, died after a few months' residence at the London Zoo. Philip Lutley Sclater, co-editor of the book in which this sensitive study by Joseph Wolf appeared, had this to say about the fate which awaited many apes snatched from their native forests: 'The efforts made in Europe to preserve the Chimpanzee and other anthropoid Apes in captivity for any length of time, have hitherto proved unavailing. Shut up by itself in a barred den, without companions of its own species, and subjected to the continual changes of climate, which occur in these latitudes, the poor captive soon withers and dies, and is replaced by another, fresh from the warm tropics, certain to undergo a similar fate in its turn.' The captors of this youngster had probably killed its mother first.

Nowadays chimpanzees flourish better in captivity than any other anthropoid ape. They are also the most intelligent of the apes, and their curiosity and manual dexterity are well known, but they are incapable of concentrating on any activity for very long. In the wild they spend most of their time gathering fruit and moving from one feeding site to another.

The true chimpanzee occupies a broad band of country from Sierra Leone on the west to the large lakes east of Zaire. The much smaller pygmy chimpanzee, *Pan paniscus*, is found in a small area in Zaire, south of the Zaire River.

Hippopotamus

HIPPOPOTAMUS, *Hippopotamus amphibius*. Hand coloured lithograph by J. Wolf, pl. 27 from his *Zoological Sketches, First Series* (edited by D. W. Mitchell and P. L. Sclater), 1861. Size of plate 13¼″ × 9″.

The hippopotamus weighs up to four tons and stands about five feet at the shoulder. Formerly widespread over much of tropical Africa it has now disappeared north of the Sahara but is still common in East Africa. When this picture was commissioned the hippopotamus was still a novel sight in Europe. The first one to be seen at the London Zoo, a male, was installed there in 1850. A female was added in 1854, bringing together the first pair to be seen in Europe since Roman times.

The unfriendly disposition of the first of these animals towards certain people was described by Philip Lutley Sclater, Secretary of the Zoological Society of London (the governing body of the London Zoo): 'There are individuals whose appearance always excites his wrath; and certain classes of persons, especially laborers and workmen wearing linen-jackets. The inveterate feeling against the latter is probably traceable to the discomfort he experienced from them at the time his present habitation was in the course of construction; his distinction of individuals is more difficult to account for. The gentleman towards whom he most constantly expresses his displeasure maintains that he never "gave his fat friend any cause of offence whatever, except that he one day addressed to him some expressions in Arabic which were certainly not complimentary."' A usually placid animal, when disturbed the hippopotamus can be aggressive and has killed many humans.

With only these two captive animals as models Joseph Wolf tried to create a realistic picture of hippopotami in the wild. The result, as with most of Wolf's imaginative wildlife scenes, was entirely satisfactory.

Giant Panda

AILUROPE, *Ailuropus melanoleucus* (now Giant Panda, *Ailuropoda melanoleuca*). Chromolithograph by G. Severeyns after an original drawing by Huet, pl. 50 from Vol. 2 (*Atlas*) of H. H. and A. Milne Edwards's *Recherches pour Servir à l'Histoire Naturelle des Mammifères*, 1868–74. Size of plate 12″ × 9¼″.

Although the giant panda seems always to have been among us it was unknown in the West until 1869 when Alphonse Milne Edwards, a naturalist working in Paris, received a letter from the French missionary Père David describing his discovery of it in the central Chinese province of Szechuan. Père David thought he had discovered a bear but it turned out to be a quite different animal, destined by its striking markings, its friendly disposition, its rarity and its vulnerability to become one of the best known of all the larger mammals. Those familiar with the illustration designed by the late Sir Peter Scott as the logo of the World Wildlife Fund may criticise this picture as being inaccurate. The criticism is justified, but there are extenuating circumstances. It is the first published picture of the giant panda and was probably based upon a preserved skin brought to Paris from Szechuan when transport was difficult and time-consuming: all things considered we should be full of praise for the artist.

The giant panda has been declining in numbers in its native bamboo forests for many years and does not breed readily in captivity. Many of us may go through life without seeing one. As no more than a thousand giant pandas were living in the wild in the early 1980s it is possible that the logo of the World Wildlife Fund, an organisation dedicated to the preservation of endangered species, could represent an extinct animal by the year 2000, less than 150 years after the first picture of it was published.

Pl. 50.

Huet. Pinx.

Chromolith. G. Severeyns

Sumatran Rhinoceros

SUMATRAN RHINOCEROS, *Rhinoceros sumatrensis* (now *Dicerorhinus sumatrensis*). Hand coloured lithograph by J. Wolf and J. Smit after a drawing by Wolf, pl. 97 from P. L. Sclater's *On the Rhinoceroses now or lately living in the Society's Menagerie* (in *Transactions of the Zoological Society of London*, Vol. 9 No. 1), 1877. Size of plate 12″ × 9½″.

Philip Lutley Sclater said he wrote his article on the rhinoceroses exhibited at one time or another in the gardens of the Zoological Society of London, 'to illustrate the very beautiful drawings by Mr Wolf'. This drawing was based on sketches made by Wolf of an old female animal purchased for the London Zoo on 2 August 1872 from William Jamrach, a dealer in exotic animals, who received £600 for it. The first Sumatran rhinoceros to be exhibited there, it had been captured in the Sunghi-njong district of Malacca on the western side of the Malayan Peninsula. It died six weeks later and after it had been stuffed it was placed in the British Museum (it is now in the Natural History Museum in London). Jamrach speedily obtained a living replacement for it which he sold to the Zoo for the same amont. Wolf's masterly drawing shows the two animals together although they never met. Under the circumstances even the cleverest use of photography could not have improved upon Wolf's imaginative juxtaposition of the two animals.

This species differs from the Indian rhinoceros in having two horns instead of one and in its smaller stature. Standing only four and a half feet at the shoulder, it is the world's smallest rhinoceros and is easily the lightest, seldom weighing more than a ton. It is also the world's hairiest rhinoceros. In large bulls the front horn may reach a length of about 20 inches, more than twice the length attained by the rear horn. Now an endangered species, the Sumatran rhinoceros lives in thick bamboo forests in Sumatra, the Malay Peninsula and Borneo.

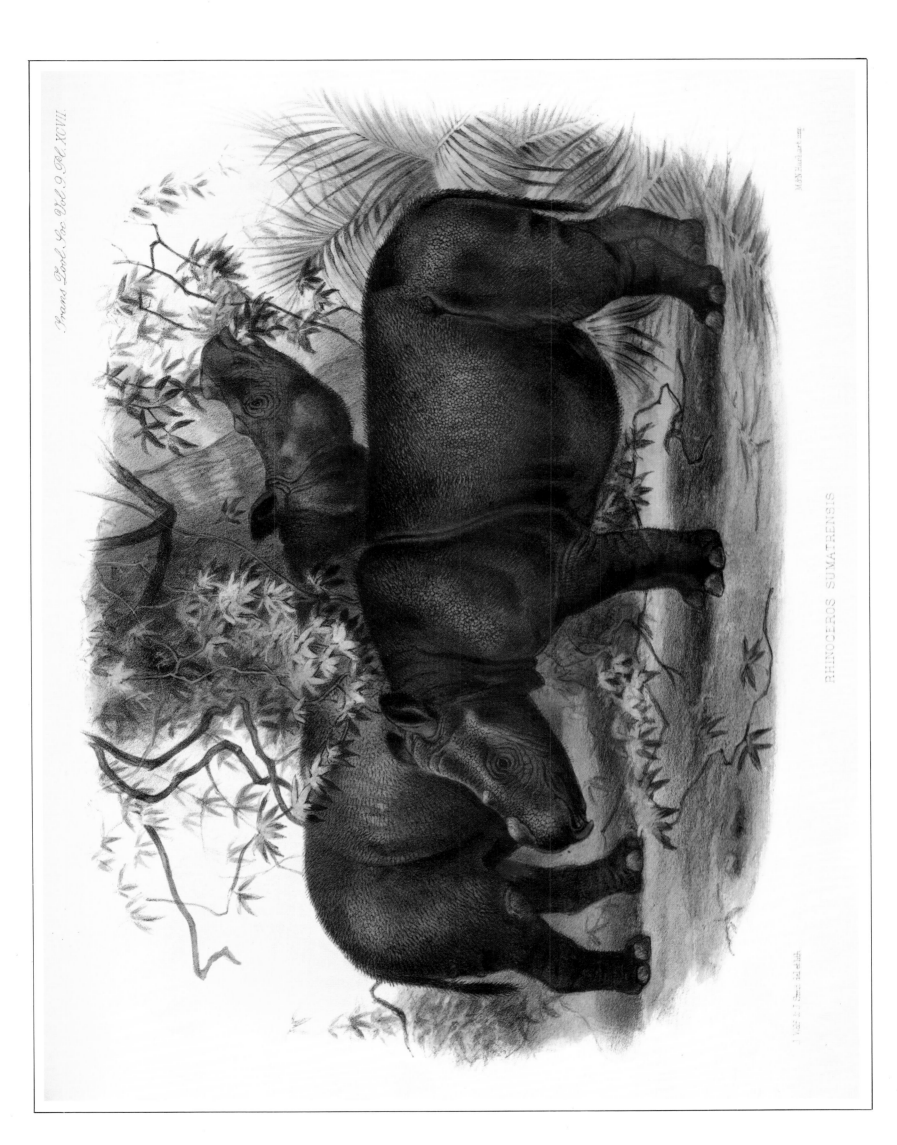

M & N Hanhart imp.

RHINOCEROS SUMATRENSIS

Caribbean Manatee

MANATEE, *Manatus australis* (now Caribbean Manatee, *Trichechus manatus*). Hand coloured lithograph by J. Smit from an original drawing by J. Wolf, pl. 7 from E. R. Alston's *Mammals* (in *Biologia Centrali Americana*, Vol. 2), 1879–82. Size of plate 12½″ × 10″.

This, the commonest of the three existing manatees, attains a length of thirteen feet and may weigh up to 1500 pounds. Already uncommon in Central America when Joseph Wolf's picture of it was published, the Caribbean manatee is now found in coastal and estuarine waters from North Carolina round to the Gulf of Mexico, the Caribbean and the Bahamas. It is herbivorous, slow moving and almost defenceless.

When moving through the water it uses its tail for propulsion and as a rudder to control pitching and rolling movements. As pictured here it rests by apparently hanging suspended near the water surface. In June 1878 a live specimen was exhibited at the Westminster Aquarium in London and it survived there until March 1879. Joseph Wolf was able to sketch it when it was alive and the drawing, as E. R. Alston says, 'well represents the curious position which that animal habitually assumed when at rest'.

A normally silent animal, the Caribbean manatee can emit high pitched screams and squeals. It is hard to understand how a creature so unprepossessing in appearance and with such a limited vocal range could have been mistaken for the mythical mermaid. Perhaps its peculiar way of taking a rest had something to do with it, or the nipples under its flippers may have reminded an onlooker of a human mother nursing her baby.

MANATUS AUSTRALIS.

Common Dolphin and Bottle-nosed Dolphin

COMMON DOLPHIN, *Delphinus delphis* (upper) and *Delphinus tursio* (lower) (now Bottle-nosed Dolphin, *Tursiops truncatus*). Hand coloured lithograph from W. H. Flower's *On the external characters of two species of British Dolphins (Delphinus delphis, Linn., and Delphinus tursio, Fabr.)* (in: *Transactions of the Zoological Society of London*, Vol. 2 Part 1), 1880. Size of plate 12½" × 9½".

The common dolphin and the bottle-nosed dolphin are now familiar from their appearances on television; and many of us have visited marine aquaria and witnessed their acrobatic performances. The common dolphin was well known to the ancient Greeks and seems to have always been with us, so it is surprising to learn that no adequate figure of it had existed in any zoological work before the upper one in this lithograph was published in 1880. The specimen which had the dubious honour of being the subject of the first adequate portrait was caught in a mackerel net off the Cornish coast in March 1879. The figure shows that it is distinguishable from the very similar but much larger bottle-nosed dolphin by its darker back and the distinct black line along its flank.

The specimen of the bottle-nosed dolphin shown here, a male not quite fully grown, was one of several captured near Holyhead, North Wales, on 5 October 1868. It is not usually as dark in colour as shown here and may have been dead for some time before the artist painted its portrait. This species may reach a length of about fourteen feet, whereas the common dolphin seldom exceeds eight feet. Both, but particularly the bottle-nosed dolphin, are highly intelligent, sociable and playful. They learn tricks rapidly, often play together, invent games of their own and give every appearance of thoroughly enjoying themselves when performing before a human audience. They may also be trained to help divers working in deep water. In the wild, however, they can be fearless in the face of danger. They have been seen to butt at the gills of a large shark which has approached a dolphin family group too closely, wounding the shark so seriously that it has died. We may be able to teach these trusting creatures a trick or two, but perhaps we should try learning a few things from them as well.

1 $\frac{1}{6}$

2 $\frac{1}{10}$

J. Smit. lith.

Hanhart imp.

1. DELPHINUS DELPHIS.   2. DELPHINUS TURSIO

Lion

LION, *Felis leo* (now *Panthera leo*). Hand coloured lithograph by J. Smit from an original drawing by J. Wolf, pl. 1 from D. G. Elliot's *A Monograph of the Felidae, or Family of the Cats*, 1883. Size of plate 23¼" × 18½".

Although this picture captures the essential physical features of the King of Beasts it conveys little of the animal's latent ferocity and power. Perhaps it tells us more about the mental attitude of the artist and the conditions under which he worked on his drawing than it tells us about lions. Joseph Wolf may have visited the Lion House at the London Zoo to make preliminary sketches for the picture. He may have seen a frog leap into their water supply, but he was in any case quite prepared to introduce this kind of whimsical touch into his studies of wild life. He knew that curiosity is a feature of cats, big and small, and that for most of the time the lion is not fierce. It is possible that Wolf had never seen one really hungry, certain that he had never seen one in the wild. Being a truthful artist he painted what he had seen, a group of well-fed, contented lions.

Lions are sociable creatures and are rarely seen on their own. A large male, easily distinguished from the female by its mane, may measure up to nine feet from nose to tail-tip and may weigh more than 400 pounds. Wolf's lions may not look fierce but they do look heavy! The lioness in the right foreground also looks powerfully muscled about the shoulders and gives the impression, rightly, that she is as accomplished a killer as the male. Indeed, lionesses kill more often than lions. In the background of Wolf's picture a lion is seen roaring, which it does mainly at sunset or just before dawn; the roar may be heard as much as five miles away.

FELIS LEO

Snow Leopard

SNOW LEOPARD, *Felis uncia* (now *Panthera uncia*). Hand coloured lithograph by J. Smit from an original drawing by J. Wolf, pl. 4 from D. G. Elliot's *A Monograph of the Felidae, or Family of the Cats*, 1883. Size of plate 23¼″ × 18½″.

This is a magnificent study of one of the handsomest of the wild cats. Joseph Wolf, famous for his studies of birds of prey, was outstanding for his life-like portrayals of wild life and he was unequalled in the nineteenth century for his ability to place his subjects in naturalistic settings. Here he evokes the spirit of place superbly even though he had never been anywhere near the mountainous regions of Central Asia, the remote haunts of the snow leopard.

With a body length of three and a half feet the three-foot-long tail looks more substantial than it is. This is because the snow leopard has exceptionally thick fur, as much as two inches thick on its back. Living mostly at altitudes between 7000 and 18,000 feet it needs thick fur if it is to stay warm. Of course it does not spend all its time at such extreme altitudes. It preys upon large and small mammals anywhere between the tree line and the snow line, as opportunity allows. In the summer it follows them as they migrate upwards to feed on the higher montane pastures. It will stalk them while they are grazing or resting and sometimes ambushes them, usually choosing the hours of twilight or darkness.

The snow leopard's beautiful fur, so attractively marked with dark grey rosettes, has always been highly prized in the fur trade and has contributed to a marked decline in its numbers in recent years. Although a protected species over much of its range, it is still hunted illegally and its pelt offered for sale.

FELIS UNCIA.

Clouded Leopard

CLOUDED TIGER, *Felis diardi* (now Clouded Leopard, *Neofelis nebulosa*). Hand coloured lithograph by J. Smit, from an original drawing by J. Wolf, pl. 8 from D. G. Elliot's *A Monograph of the Felidae, or Family of the Cats,* 1883. Size of plate 23¼″ × 18½″.

Possibly the most strikingly marked of all the larger cats, the clouded leopard is a forest dweller, sleeping in a tree during the day and hunting at night. Because of its nocturnal habits we know little about its habits in the wild, though we do know that it feeds on monkeys, birds, deer and other small mammals. Using its long and heavy tail as a balancer, it climbs trees easily and seems to be most at home where the jungle is thickest.

As with other cats the spots and blotches decorating its fur seem to be an adaptation to a forest existence and presumably help to make it inconspicuous. Not surprisingly this handsome animal has been hunted for its fur and its numbers are declining. It used to be widespread in south-eastern Asia, but the destruction of suitable habitats in some parts of its range, especially in Malaysia and Thailand, has also contributed to its decline. Fortunately it breeds readily in captivity and may be seen in the larger zoos of the world. The clouded leopard is distinct enough from the larger cats, such as the lion and the tiger, and the smaller cats, such as the ocelot and the bobcat, to have been placed in a genus of its own, *Neofelis*.

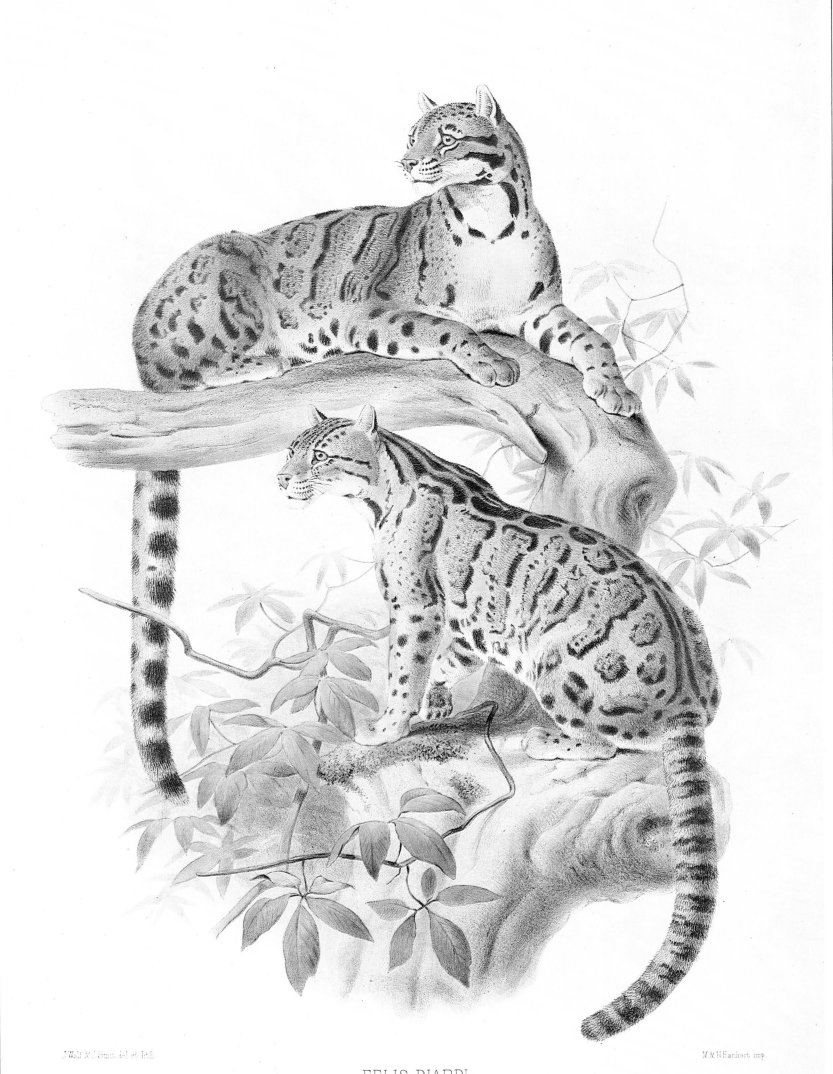

FELIS DIARDI.

Serval

SERVAL, *Felis serval*. Hand coloured lithograph by J. Smit, from an original drawing by J. Wolf, pl. 26 from D. G. Elliot's *A Monograph of the Felidae, or Family of the Cats*, 1883. Size of plate 23¼″ × 18½″.

Daniel Giraud Elliot, a wealthy American businessman with an enthusiasm for wildlife, commissioned Joseph Wolf to provide original coloured drawings for *A Monograph of the Felidae* and for several lavishly illustrated books about birds. Happily Elliot gave Wolf a free hand and the resulting illustrations include some of the finest wildlife compositions published in the nineteenth century, those in the Felidae monograph being among the most outstanding portrayals of mammals by any artist.

The serval is a slender, long-legged creature, three feet in length plus a foot-long tail. The small head has large ears which are usually seen set wider apart than those of the animal facing us in Wolf's picture. Its fawn coat, ornamented with longitudinal rows of black spots, helps make it inconspicuous in the grassy scrub country which it frequents. A darker form with small, more densely crowded spots was once considered to be a separate species, known as the servaline cat, *Felis servalina*. The serval occurs widely in Africa, the variety being limited to western Africa. One of the faster wild cats, the serval feeds mostly on rodents.

FELIS SERVAL

Husky Dog

ESQUIMAUX DOG, *Canis familiaris* var. (now Husky Dog, *Canis familiaris*).
Hand coloured lithograph by J. G. Keulemans, pl. 38 from St George
Mivart's *Dogs, Jackals, Wolves and Foxes: a Monograph of the Canidae*, 1890.
Size of plate 10″ × 7½″.

The husky dog is classed among the domestic dogs although, like the
alsatian, it is derived mostly from the wolf, *Canis lupus*. It is still largely
a wild dog, retaining much of the appearance and character of its ancestors,
and is valued for its ability to work rather than for its submissive qualities. St
George Mivart says that 'a pack of them was once mistaken for wolves even
by so experienced an Arctic traveller as Sir John Richardson'. Eskimos and
the earlier polar explorers tried to impose their will on huskies by subjecting
them to needlessly harsh and cruel treatment, so the dogs did not give of
their best. There has been little selective breeding of huskies with special
aptitude for work, but they do reward kind treatment with better service.

$\frac{1}{6}$

J. G. Keulemans del. et lith.

THE ESQUIMAUX DOG.

Canis familiaris, var.

Mintern Bros. imp.

Mexican Lap-dog

MEXICAN LAP-DOG, *Canis familiaris* var. (now *Canis familiaris*). Hand coloured lithograph by J. G. Keulemans, pl. 39 from St George Mivart's *Dogs, Jackals, Wolves and Foxes: a Monograph of the Canidae*, 1890. Size of plate 10″ × 7½″.

The artist John Gerrard Keulemans, perhaps better known for his studies of exotic birds, prepared this illustration from a stuffed dog housed in the Natural History Museum in London. The dog measured only seven inches from the end of its snout to the root of its tail, making it one of the smallest known. Little dogs, such as the Chihuahua, have been bred in Mexico for centuries, but only recently as pets. To the Aztecs, for instance, the little creatures were appreciated as delicacies for the dinner table and valued in magic, burial rites and medicine.

St George Mivart contrasted the Mexican lap-dog with the Esquimaux dog and said that it had most probably been formed from dogs of European origin. So impressed was he with the variety of breeds of domestic dog that he was moved to say, 'it is absolutely the most wonderful species of animal known to us as regards the number and diversity of the races which compose it.' Many dog lovers will agree with him.

$$\frac{3}{4}$$

THE MEXICAN LAP-DOG.
Canis familiaris, *var.*

Black Wildebeest

WHITE-TAILED GNU, *Connochaetes gnu* (now Black Wildebeest, *Connochaetes gnou*). Hand coloured lithograph by J. Smit, pl. 12 from Vol. 1 of P. L. Sclater and O. Thomas's *The Book of Antelopes*, 1894–1900. Size of plate 11″ × 8½″.

The black wildebeest used to be abundant over much of South Africa but the hunting and agricultural activities of European colonists almost exterminated it. Conservation measures have halted the carnage and increased its chances of survival. This is not the animal featured in television programmes undertaking its dramatic seasonal migrations, thundering along in countless thousands; that animal is the larger blue wildebeest, *Connochaetes taurinus*. The black wildebeest, which numbered less than 4000 examples in 1970, was first seen in Europe in 1776 but was rare in European zoos until the late nineteenth century.

Grant's Gazelle

GRANT'S GAZELLE, *Gazella granti*. Hand coloured lithograph by J. Smit from an original drawing by J. Wolf, pl. 69 from Vol. 2 of P. L. Sclater and O. Thomas's *The Book of Antelopes*, 1894–1900. Size of plate 11″ × 8½″.

This lithograph of a Joseph Wolf watercolour drawing enables us to see at once why Grant's gazelle, a model of symmetry distinguished above all by the beautiful lines of its massive horns, is generally considered to be one of the most beautiful of the antelopes. In 1860, during their exploration of Central Africa, John Speke and James Grant were detained for a long time at Ugogo (in what is now Tanzania) by the drunken native chief Magombo. It was then the explorers first met with the animal that would one day be named after one of them. A creature of the open plains, Grant's gazelle is found in East Africa on each side of the Equator.

European Bison

EUROPEAN BISON, *Bos bonasus* (now *Bison bonasus*). Hand coloured lithograph by J. Smit, pl. 5 from R. Lydekker's *Wild Oxen, Sheep, & Goats of all Lands, Living and Extinct*, 1898. Size of plate 11½″ × 8½″.

When this lithograph was published the European bison still occurred in the wild in Russia; a large group existed in the Bialowiecza Forest and another in the Caucasus. Formerly protected by Tsar Alexander I, the first group was annihilated during the First World War and the second did not survive beyond 1927. Fortunately a number had been placed in zoos and with three survivors of a wild population a successful breeding programme was instituted. This ensured that the European bison would survive, and it is now resident in many zoos. It has been re-introduced into the Bialowiecza Forest and elsewhere in Russia and Romania.

Originally this large and heavy mammal lived in woodland areas where it ate leaves, ferns, heather, shrubs and bark. Otherwise, little is known about its behaviour in the wild. In Richard Lydekker's book, from which our picture is taken, we learn that these animals 'dearly love a mud-bath, and at times when the flies are troublesome they may frequently be seen plastered over with a coat of dry mud, which forms an efficient protection against their tormentors'. The European bison has longer legs, a smaller head, a longer body and a shorter mane than the American bison. It is also more wary but shares with its American cousin a good sense of smell and poor eyesight.

EUROPEAN BISON.

Published by Rowland Ward Ltd

Markhor

MARKHOR, *Capra falconeri*. Hand coloured lithograph after an original drawing by J. Wolf, pl. 25 from R. Lydekker's *Wild Oxen, Sheep, & Goats of all Lands*, 1898. Size of plate 11½″ × 8½″.

The largest and, to the sportsman at least, the handsomest of the wild goats, the markhor is notable for the variations in the form of its horns, which have been used by some authorities to help define several subspecies of this animal. The variations in the spiral conformation are particularly striking and some pairs of horns show a much more closely wound spiral than those in this picture by Joseph Wolf. As its horns are among the most coveted of all hunting trophies the markhor has been exterminated in many parts of its range.

Standing about 40 inches high at the shoulder and weighing 200 pounds or more, these noble creatures inhabit precipitous and broken ground in arid parts of the Himalayas from Kashmir to Afghanistan, just above the tree line. They are very agile, may congregate in herds and in some places have been seen feeding together with the ibex, *Capra ibex*.

The name markhor means 'snake-eater' in Persian but there is no evidence to suggest that it feeds on snakes. Curiously enough a propensity for eating snakes was once said to be an attribute of the common goat in Scotland, Both animals, of course, are grazers.

ASTOR MARKHOR.

Published by Rowland Ward Ltd.

Okapi

OKAPI, *Okapia johnstoni*. Hand coloured lithograph by P. J. Smit, pl. 30 from
E. Ray Lankester's *On Okapia, a new genus of Giraffidae, from Central Africa*
(in *Transactions of the Zoological Society of London* Vol. 16), 1902. Size of plate
12″ × 9½″.

This is a remarkable and historic picture of a large African mammal;
remarkable because it is an artist's reconstruction, historic because it is
the first published picture of the okapi. Two strips of skin had been obtained
by Sir Harry Johnston during a visit to the Congo Free State in 1900 and
these were enough for Philip Lutley Sclater to rush into print with the
description of a new species of horse, *Equus johnstoni*. Subsequently Johnston
received a complete skin and two skulls. These remains enabled Professor E.
Ray Lankester, then Director of the Natural History Museum in London, to
write an informed article about the exciting new discovery, which turned
out to be like a short-necked giraffe with striped hindquarters, a wonderful
addition to the pantheon of African wildlife. Smit's fine lithograph illustrating the article proved to be an accurate representation of the okapi when live
specimens finally reached the West.

Slender evidence of the okapi's existence had been given in H. M.
Stanley's book *In Darkest Africa*, published in 1890. Speaking of the pygmies
in the Ituri forests of the Congo he had written: 'The Wambutti knew a
donkey and called it "atti". They say that they sometimes catch them in pits.'
This, and a discussion with Stanley himself, had been enough to set Johnston
on the trail that eventually led him to the okapi.

Mintern Bros. imp.

P.J. Smit del. et lith.

THE OKAPI (OKAPIA JOHNSTONI)

Crested Porcupine

CRESTED PORCUPINE, *Hystrix cristata*. Chromolithograph by P. J. Smit, pl. 55 from J. Anderson's *Zoology of Egypt. Mammalia*, 1902. Size of plate 12¼″ × 9½″.

The crested porcupine, a large rodent about two feet long and weighing about 60 pounds, is remarkable for its crest of white-tipped grey quills. These quills, supplemented by others which are hollow and open at their ends, are loosely attached to the animal and are easily detached, from which circumstance arose the early and erroneous belief that they could be ejected like darts and used as offensive weapons. When attacked the animal may do no more than charge backwards with its spines erect. The effect, however, can be intimidating and painful. Even the lion learns to treat it respectfully.

Although this picture is an illustration from a book about Egyptian mammals it is unlikely that the crested porcupine still exists in Egypt. It does occur elsewhere in Africa, however, and is common across the central part of the continent. In some places it is all too common and has become a pest to crops. As it is hunted for food and for its quills it may not be a pest for much longer. It may owe its limited occurrence in Europe to introductions by man, probably the Romans. When first seen in Italy it would have seemed a delightfully exotic creature. Unfortunately it has become scarce there now.

Pl. LV.

HYSTRIX CRISTATA.

Harp Seal

HARP OR GREENLAND SEAL, *Phoca groenlandica* (now Harp Seal, *Phoca groenlandica*). Colour print after an original painting by J. G. Millais, pl. 35 from Vol. 1 of his *Mammals of Great Britain and Ireland*, 1904–1906. Size of plate 10¼″ × 8″.

The harp seal is one of the smaller seals, measuring five or six feet long when adult. John Guille Millais says it may weigh 'as much as 800 pounds', but it does not normally exceed 300 pounds. Its striking colour pattern of yellowish-white with a contrasting broad black band makes it easy to identify. The black marking on its back recalls the shape of a harp and explains the derivation of its name.

The alternative name, Greenland seal, indicates this animal's preference for living under arctic conditions. Millais gives a graphic picture of its chosen domain. 'The home of the Harp Seal', he writes, 'is near the bleak shores of Greenland and the polar islands, forlorn regions of dreary waste where the accumulations of centuries of winters have formed fields of ice, topped by glittering heights. Near such lands the Greenland seal loves to lie close to the open cracks in the floes, or to fish in the surrounding depths. Its enemies are the Eskimo hunter, the white man from St John's, Trondhjem, Copenhagen, and Dundee, the polar bear, the shark, the swordfish and perhaps the orca [killer whale]; and yet despite the toll these take, it is only the fringe of the great multitudes that are molested. Imagine the abundance of a species of which 200,000 are annually killed in one small area, to the north of St John's, and there is no diminution. Yet it is so.' Millais wrote about the persecution of the harp seal at the beginning of the twentieth century: had he been writing towards its close how different may have been his conclusion!

Polecat

POLECAT, *Putorius putorius* (now *Mustela putorius*). Chromolithograph after a painting by A. Thorburn, pl. 22 from Vol. 2 of J. G. Millais' *Mammals of Great Britain and Ireland*, 1904–06. Size of plate 10¼″ × 8″.

The polecat is one of many small, short-legged, elongated animals comprising the Mustelidae, the family which also includes the badger, otter, weasel, pine marten, stoat and mink. It attains a length of about two feet, has small eyes set in a flattened triangular head and is noteworthy for its cream-coloured fur partially obscured by long, black-tipped hairs, these being densest on the belly. This coloration is acquired when the animal is about eight months old, the fur of the youngsters being much paler.

It is bold but careless, which makes it easy to trap. As it is very destructive to small domestic and farmyard animals, such as pigeons, rabbits, hens and chickens, it has been killed in large numbers and is now very scarce or absent from some areas where it was once common, such as Britain. According to John Guille Millais, the author of the impressive three-volume work in which this study of the polecat appears, 'It will attack even so large a bird as a turkey and has been known to kill 16 in one night. One has been seen to attack and hold a fully grown Hare.' It may sometimes be a benefactor to man as it is also known to destroy venomous snakes and vermin such as rats and mice. More than most creatures of its size the polecat loves to kill. Archibald Thorburn's picture shows how handsome is the coat of this efficient little predator, handsome enough to have been used formerly to adorn civic robes in England.

Blue Whale and Fin Whale

BLUE WHALE, *Balaenoptera musculus* (top), Common Rorqual, *Balaenoptera physalus* (centre and bottom) (now Fin Whale). Coloured print by J. G. Millais, pl. 59 from Vol. 3 of J. G. Millais' *The Mammals of Great Britain and Ireland*, 1904–06. Size of plate 10¼″ × 8″.

Like most early illustrations of whales this one shows them with distended bellies: but, except when feeding, their bellies are flat. Only dead whales would have distended bellies, as shown here, and usually they would have been the victims of whalers. The fin whale was not hunted – and so was not accessible to artists – until the problem of making it float when dead had been solved (by pumping compressed air into its carcase). The top figure in this illustration by John Guille Millais (the fourth son of Sir John Everett Millais) shows an example of the largest animal the world has ever seen. All the statistics of the blue whale are impressive, sometimes staggering. It reaches 110 feet in length and may weigh 140 tonnes. As it surfaces it blasts out a steaming mixture of moisture-laden mucus and trapped water from the blowhole situated on the top of its head, the 'spout' sometimes rising as high as 33 feet and often being characteristic enough to allow positive identification. The stomach may contain a ton or more of krill (a mixture of mature and larval forms of shrimps, crabs and other invertebrates) and several tons may be taken in daily. There are from 60 to 100 grooves on the throat and chest, each groove being about two inches deep. Despite its great size the blue whale is an efficient swimmer and may briefly reach a speed of 15 knots. Regrettably this friendly monster is in danger of being exterminated. In every sense its demise would be a great loss.

The other two figures represent the fin whale, a species which occasionally attains a length of 80 feet and a weight of 60 tonnes. As its blubber is thinner than that of the blue whale it was hunted less vigorously – until the larger species became scarce. It was known to the early whalemen as Razorback because of the pronounced ridge along its back.

1.   THE BLUE WHALE.
Balænoptera musculus.

2, 3. THE COMMON RORQUAL.
Balænoptera physalus.

INDEX

Adams, A. 72
Ailuropoda melanoleuca 92, 93
Alces alces 10, 11
Alouatta seniculus 86, 87
Alston, E.R. 96
Anderson, J. 34
Annedouche 48
Anteater, marsupial 34, 35
Audebert, Jean Baptiste 12
Audubon, John James 5, 6, 7, 66, 68

Bachman, Revd John 6, 7, 66, 68
Balaenoptera musculus 126, 127
Balaenoplera physalus 126, 127
Bear, brown 46, 47
Bison bonasus 114, 115
Bison, European 114, 115
Bos taurus 52, 53
Brown, Captain Thomas 36
Buffalo, African 44, 45
Burmeister, C.H.C. 80

Camel, Bactarian 5, 18, 19
Camelus bactiranus 18, 19
Capri nubiana 24, 25
Capybara 7, 28, 29
Cassin, J. 82
Cattle, Hereford 52, 53
Cat, wild 32, 33
Chimpanzee 88, 89
Chrysocyou brachyurus 80, 81
Couepatus mesoleucus 56, 57
Coutant 22
Couzens, Charles 56
Cuscus, spotted 22, 23
Cuvier, G.F. 5, 14, 18, 20

Deer, mule 82, 83
de Last, C. 18, 20
Delphinapterus leucas 30, 31
Delphinus delphis 98, 99
de Saint-Vincent, Bory 32
Dicerorhinus sumatrensis 94, 95
Dickes, W. 34
Dog, husky 108, 109
Dog, Mexican lap- 110, 111
Dolphin, bottle-nosed 98, 99
Dolphin, common 98, 99
Dumenil, A. 46
Du Petit-Thouars, A. 46
Dürer, Albrecht 5

Edwards, H.H. and A. Milne 92
Ehrenberg, Christian Gottfried 5, 24
Eland 74, 75
Elephant, African 38, 39
Elephant, Asiatic 38, 39
Elephas maximus 38, 39
Elliot, Daniel Giraud 6, 100, 102, 104, 106
Equus burchelli burchelli 76, 77
Equus caballus 50, 51
Equus quagga 20, 21
Erinaceus europaeus 8, 9
Eydoux, J.F.T. 48

Felis coucolor 26, 27
Felis sevral 106, 107
Felis silvestus 32, 33
Flower, W.H. 98
Flying fox, grey-headed 64, 65
Flying squirrel, northern 70, 71
François 32
Fraser, Louis 56

Gaimard, J.P. 22
Gazella granti 112, 113
Gazelle, Grant's 112, 113
Gemsbok 42, 43
Gessner, Conrad 5
Giraffa camelopardalis 36, 37
Giraffe 36, 37
Glaucomys sabrinus 70, 71
Gorilla, Lowland 7
Gorilla 78, 79
Gorilla gorilla 78, 79
Gould John 6, 58, 60, 62, 64
Gray, John Edward 72, 74
Guanaco 74, 75

Harris, Capt. W. Cornwallis 42, 44
Hawkins, Benjamin Waterhouse 6, 74, 76
Hedgehog, European 8, 9
Hippopotamus 90, 91
Hippopotamus amphibius 90, 91
Horse, Arab 50, 51
Howard, Frank 42, 44
Huet 92
Hydrochoerus hydrochaeris 28, 29
Hystrix cristata 120, 121

Ibex, Nubian 5, 24, 25

Keuleman, J.G. 6
Koala 58, 59
Kudu, greater 40, 41

Lama guanicoe 74, 75
Lankester, E. Ray 118
Lemur catta 12, 13
Lemur, ring-tailed 12, 13
Leontopithecus chrysomelas 16, 17
Leopard, clouded 104, 105
Leopard, snow 102, 103
Lion 100, 101
Lizars, W.H. 5, 26, 28, 30
Low David 6, 7, 50, 52, 54
Loxodouta africana 38, 39
Lydekker, R. 114, 116

Macropus robustus 62m 63
Manatee, Caribbean 96, 97
Maréchal, Nicolas 20
Markhor 116, 117
Millais, John Guille 122, 124, 126
Miller, John Frederick 10
Milne, S 38
Mivart, St. George 108
Monkey, Red Howler 86, 87
Moose 10, 11
Mosses, A. 28
Mustela franata 68, 69
Mustela putorius 124, 125
Myrmecobius fasciatus 34, 35

Neofelis nebulosa 104, 105
Nicholson, W. 50, 52, 54
Numbat 34, 35

Odocoileus hemiones 82, 83
Okapi 7, 118, 119
Okapia johnstoni 118, 119
Orang utan 72, 73
Oryx gazella 42, 43
Ovis aries 54, 55
Owen, Richard 78

Panda, giant 6, 7, 92, 93
Panthera leo 100, 101
Panthera uncia 102, 103
Pan troglodytes 88, 89
Peale, T.R. 82
Phalanger maculatis 22, 23
Phascolarctos cinereus 58, 59
Phloemys cumingi 48, 49
Phoca groenlandica 122, 123
Pongo pygmaeus 72, 73
Porcupine, crested 120, 121
Prévost 22
Pteropus poliocephalus 64, 65
Puma 26, 27

Quagga 20, 21
Quoy, J.R.C. 22

Rat, slender-tailed cloud 48, 49
Rhinoceros, Indian 14, 15
Rhinoceros, Sumatran 6, 94, 95
Rhinoceros unicornis 14, 15
Richter, H.C. 50, 60, 62, 64

Saint-Hilaire, E. Geoffroy 5, 14, 18, 20
Saint-Hilaire, Isidore Geoffrey 32, 46
Sclater, Philip Lutley 88, 90, 94
Seal, harp 122, 123
Seba, Albert 5, 8
Serval 106, 107
Severeyns, G. 92
Sheep, Lincoln, long wooled 54, 55
Sheils, William 50, 52
Skunk, hog-nosed 56
Sloth, pale-throated 6, 84, 85
Smith, Andrew 40
Smit, P.J. 7, 94, 96, 100, 102, 104, 106, 112, 114, 118, 120
Souleyet, F.A. 48
Syme, Patrick 30
Synceros caffer 44, 45

Tamarin, golden-headed 16, 17
Tamias stinatus 66, 67
Tanjé, P. 8
Thomas, O. 112
Thorburn, Archibald 124
Thylacine 60, 61
Thylacinus cynocephalus 60, 61
Tragelaphus oryx 74, 75
Tragelaphus strepsiceros 40, 41
Trichechus manatus 96, 97
Tursiops truncatus 98, 99

Ursus arctos 46, 47

Wallaroo 62, 63
Warwick, W. 36
Water-hog 28, 29
Waterhouse, George R. 34
Weasel, long-tailed 68, 69
Werner, J. 18, 20, 32, 46, 48
Whale, white 30, 31
Wied-Neuwied, Prince Maximilian Alexander Philipp of 16
Wildebeest, black 112, 113
Wilson, James 5, 26, 28
Wing, W. 72
Wolf, J. 6, 7, 78, 88, 90, 94, 96, 100, 102, 104, 106, 112, 116
Wolf, maned 80, 81

Zebra, Burchell's 76, 77